EDITOR: LEE J(

C000230802

THE BORDER REIVERS

Text by
KEITH DURHAM
Colour plates by
ANGUS McBRIDE

First published in Great Britain in 1995 by
Osprey, an imprint of Reed Consumer Books Ltd.
Michelin House, 81 Fulham Road,
London SW3 6RB
and Auckland, Melbourne, Singapore and Toronto

ISBN 1 85532 560 8

Filmset in Great Britain
Printed through World Print Ltd, Hong Kong

Museums

For those readers seeking additional information on
this subject the following museums are recom-
mended:

    The Border History Museum, Hexham.
    Tullie House, Carlisle.
    Museum of Border Arms and Armour,
      Teviotdale.
    Kelvin Grove Museum, Glasgow.

Author's Dedication

This book is dedicated to the memory of my friend,
Rick Scollins, 1946–1992.

Acknowledgements

I would like to thank the following for their generous
assistance and courtesy. Brian Moffat and his family,
'Museum of Border Arms and Armour', Teviotdale;
The Border History Museum, Hexham; Peter Dougal,
for sustained encouragement; Jean Shaw, for typing the
manuscript; Pete Armstrong, for his fine pen and ink
drawings; John Tincey; Steve Laws; Gateshead Central
Library; The Tower of London Armouries; British
Library; Historic Scotland; M.P.S. Photographic,
Newcastle; and John Marsden, historian.

Publisher's Note

Readers may wish to study this title in conjunction with
the following Osprey publications:
    MAA 191 *Henry VIII's Army*
    MAA 256 *The Irish Wars 1485–1603*

Edwin's Kingdom

For details of this popular series of videos on the
history and scenery of Northumberland and the
Borders contact:
    Hartnell Images
    PO Box 97
    Morpeth
    Northumberland
    NE61 1EU

THE BORDER REIVERS

INTRODUCTION: THE BORDER

The line of the Anglo-Scottish Border roughly follows the trend of the Cheviot Hills, that is north-east to south-west. From Berwick-upon-Tweed to the Solway Firth it wanders diagonally across the narrow neck of Britain, crossing some of the wildest and most beautiful country in the British Isles.

It is a richly varied landscape made up of bleak salt marshes, deserted beaches and fertile coastal plains; broad rivers and tumbling burns give life and colour to green wooded valleys; spongy mosses, bent grass and peat bogs surround the rocky outcrops which thrust through vast tracts of heather-covered moorland; and always on the horizon are the endless, rolling Cheviot Hills, which form the main barrier between the two countries and give the Borderland its distinctive character.

It is also a landscape which is constantly punctu-

Bleak, lonely and difficult of access, the Cheviot hills proved a formidable obstacle to the invading armies of both England and Scotland. To the Borderers, however, these bare hills and twisting passes were familiar terrain. As the Border Wars intensified and raiding became a way of life, the reivers became skilled at navigating the 'wastes' and invariably eluded the forces of law and order sent against them.

ated by reminders of fiercer times than ours. A multitude of Iron Age hill-forts overlook extensive Roman remains and Hadrian's Wall strides uncompromisingly from Wallsend to the Solway Firth. The great castles of Alnwick, Bamburgh, Caerlaverock and Carlisle stand here; and alongside them lie the silent battlefields of Otterburn, Solway Moss and Flodden Field; gaunt towers such as Smailholm, Elsdon, Oakwood and the Hollows still survive and, scattered across its hills and dales are squat bastles and peles with archaic names – Black Middens, Raw and the Hole. Starkly picturesque, they are grim reminders that this narrow stretch of land was a medieval frontier of great military importance and has a savage and turbulent history. For, as the buffer zone between two of history's most fractious neighbours, this land became their battleground and the effect of their constant warring was to leave an indelible mark on the Border folk, creating a society that, by the beginning of the 16th century, had become a dangerous thorn in the side of both nations.

For those men belonged to the great riding families; and with 'lang spear' and 'steill bonnet', they 'rode with the moonlight' and plundered the Borderland. Sporting such names as Nebless Clem, Ill Drooned Geordie, Jok Pott the Bastard, Fyre-the-Braes, Pikehood, Wynking Will and Buggerback, they were Armstrongs, Grahams, Bells, Charltons, Robsons, Nixons, Maxwells, Scotts, Milburns and others – history remembers them as the Border Reivers.

Map of the Border country, 16th–17th centuries.

'A perverse and crooked people'

With the exception of Berwick-upon-Tweed, which became part of England after its capture by Richard the Third in 1482, the Border line has remained more or less constant since the 11th and 12th centuries. After the Battle of Carham in 1018 the victorious Scots claimed all land north of the Tweed on the eastern side, and later, in 1157, William Rufus incorporated Cumberland, formerly part of Strathclyde, into England on the west, building Carlisle Castle to defend it.

Although the Borderline was constantly disputed, bearing in mind what was to come, relatively peaceful times followed. The two nations, however, continued to regard each other with suspicion and in order to install a bulwark against the ever-present threat of invasion, both governments actively encouraged settlement of their Border districts, offering

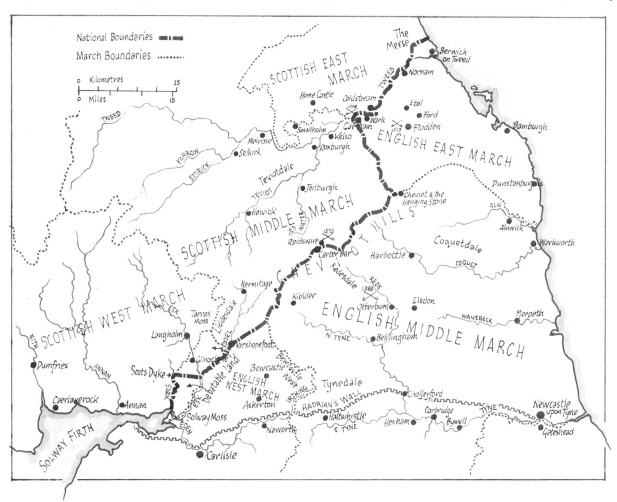

A woodcut from Holinshed's 'Chronicle' depicting a foray or raid in Northumberland. The reivers, wearing burgonets and carrying Border lances, swords and calivers, drive off cattle, sheep and valuable horses. Such raids took place with monotonous regularity, invariably provoking similar reprisals and perpetuating the recurrent cycle of violence in the Borders.

land and low rents in exchange for military service, when required. As a consequence, the countryside became heavily populated, much more so than it is today.

Overpopulation was further aggravated by a system of inheritance known as 'gavelkind', whereby a dead man's land was apportioned in equal measures amongst his sons. In the case of large families, this practice often resulted in the inheritance of meagre strips of land which could not adequately support a man and his dependants. This state of affairs, combined with a lack of legitimate alternative occupations, soon gave rise to an ever-growing delinquent element in Border society. Theft became endemic and whilst travelling through the Borderland in 1547 Andrew Boorde, an English physician, noted that the country 'lay in much poverty and penury and that there were many outlaws and strong thieves, for much of their living standeth by stealing and robbing'.

In spite of national differences, families on either side of the Border had much in common. Living off a harsh land with an inhospitable climate nurtured a tough, insular and contentious people.

A hardy mixture of landowners, tenants and hill farmers, they were it seems 'not aquainted with many learned or rare phrazes', and it took little to offend them. Law and order in the form of central government was far away, and more often than not when a dispute did arise between them 'They expect no lawe but bang it out bravely, one and his kindred against the other and his; they will subject themselves to no

justice, but in an inhumane and barbarous manner fight and kill one another; they run together in clangs [clans] as they term it, or names. This fighting they call Feides, or deadley Feides [feuds].'

Religion, it would seem, did not prove to be a moderating influence on their behaviour either. 'Amongst these rude and superstitious people even the priests went with sword and dagger' and many Border churches were, by necessity, strongly fortified. What religion they did acknowledge was of the strictly practical kind. The Scottish historian, Bishop Leslie, whose history of Scotland was written between 1572–76, tells us that their devotion to their rosaries was never greater than before setting out on a raid, and on the Scottish Border it was the custom at christening to leave unblest the child's master hand in order that unhallowed blows could be struck upon the enemy!

In an attempt to regulate and govern the Border region more effectively, the two governments had reached an agreement in 1249 known as the Laws of the Marches. By its terms both sides of the Border were divided into three areas – East, West and Middle Marches – each to be administered both judicially and militarily by a March Warden, the first being appointed in 1297.

The Border Marches

The English East March, incorporating most of north Northumberland, stretched from the North Sea to the Hanging Stone on Cheviot. For much of its length, the Borderline here follows the Tweed and its fords were defended on the English side by the castles of Wark and Norham. Berwick, which was the residence of the Warden and the 'utmost towne in England', was well fortified and described as 'the strongest holde in all Britain'. On the Scottish side, the Wardenship was usually held by the Home family who, from their fortress at Home Castle, guarded the richly fertile coastal plain known as the Merse. Due to the broad flatness of the coastal terrain, both East Marches offered an easy passage for invading armies and as a consequence suffered the thrust of many Royal incursions.

Extending from the Hanging Stone to Kershopefoot in Liddesdale, the English Middle March included Tynedale, where Hexham had the dubious distinction of being home to the first pur-pose-built prison in England, and Redesdale, which was a 'wild and unruly' district where the 'Kings writ did not run'. For defence, it relied largely on its string of castles and towers on the River Coquet, stretching from Harbottle to Warkworth. Its War-dens, who, over time, included members of the Forster, Bowes, Eure and Percy families, resided at Alnwick or at Harbottle. The English Middle March was also protected to some degree by the Cheviots which made the passage of artillery difficult but

proved no obstacle to raiders who knew the 'wastes', passes or 'ingates', of which there were over 40.

Facing this was the Scottish Middle March. Incorporating the Sheriffdoms of Selkirk, Roxburgh and Peebles, its judicial centre was Jedburgh where justice courts were held, and its Wardens, usually Kerrs, resided at their castles of Ferniehurst and Cessford. The Scottish Middle March was also the home of the notorious 'Limmers' or thieves of Teviotdale and Liddesdale. Infested with towers and 'strong houses' these grim little valleys were home to the Scotts, Elliots and Armstrongs, 'great surnames and most offensive to England', and it was men of these families who persistently launched some of the largest and most devastating raids into the English East and Middle Marches. No-one was safe from their plundering, Scots or English, and redress was hard to obtain.

Remote and inaccessible, Liddesdale in particu-lar was a veritable robbers' roost and the blatant lawlessness of its inhabitants necessitated the ap-pointment of an additional Warden, or Keeper. Re-siding in the forbidding and gloomy fortress of Her-mitage Castle, 'the strength of Liddesdale', these Keepers, at the end of the 16th century, included the likes of James Hepburn, 4th Earl of Bothwell, and Sir Walter Scott of Buccleuch, dangerous rogues who were, more often than not, in deep collusion with the thieves and raiders they were charged to control, and 'wynked' at their nightly depredations.

Incorporating Cumberland and Westmorland, the English West March ran from Kershopefoot along the Liddel Water to the Esk and down to the Solway Firth. Like the East Marches, the flat nature of the land provided a route for large-scale invasion, though the treacherous mosses and tides of the Sol-way made such enterprises a risky business, as armies of both sides found to their cost. Along with Naworth Castle, Carlisle was the key to the west door of England. A formidable castle, it was 'fortified with

A ballade of the scottysshe kynge.

An early 16th century woodcut from John Skelton's 'Ballade of the Scottyshe Kynge'. The Knight at left is heavily armoured in the Gothic style whilst, with the emphasis on manoeuvrability, the light horseman on the right wears an open helmet with cheek defences, a studded brigandine over a mail shirt and carries an eight-foot lance or 'stave'. At Flodden, many of Dacre's Border horse would have been similarly equipped. (British Library)

strong walls of stone' and was the seat of the Warden. This office was usually held by the Dacres and in later years by the Lords Scrope. Guarding the wastes to the north were Askerton, Scaleby and Bewcastle. Bewcastle, in particular, which stood in 'wild and solitarie country', was situated close to routes favoured by Liddesdale raiders, and its Captain was ever busy.

The Scottish West March comprised the Stewartries of Kirkudbright and Annandale, and included the Sheriffdom of Dumfries which served as both its judicial centre and the headquarters of the Warden, an office often held by members of the powerful Maxwell family. Its strength lay in the castles of Caerlaverock, a Maxwell stronghold situated at the mouth of the Nith, and Lochmaben, both fortresses being surrounded by a formidable system of moats. In addition, a Captain known as the Keeper of Annandale served at Langholm Castle, his duties being similar to those of his English counterpart at Bewcastle.

Lying on the boundary of these two Marches, and worthy of special mention, was the Debateable Land. Bounded by the rivers Sark, Lyne and Liddel Water, it was a tract of ground about twelve miles long by three and a half to five miles wide, its small area belying the enormous amount of grief it caused to both nations. First named in a truce document of 1450, the land was recognised as belonging to neither one side nor the other, and it had become the custom for both Scots and English to pasture their sheep and cattle on it. However, as soon as anyone attempted to erect a building, temporary or otherwise, violent disputes arose. As neither country acknowledged responsibility for the actions of the inhabitants, justice was non-existent. Not surprisingly these conditions proved extremely attractive to the lawless elements in the Western Marches and it soon became a sanctuary for fugitives, 'broken men' (outlaws) and murderers. It also attracted Armstrongs, Littles, Bells and the predatory Grahams, who were 'very famous among the Borderers for their martiall disposition'. Taking full advantage of the situation, they used the Debateable Land as a base for their marauding and became equally famous for the fine impartiality with which they plundered and murdered Scots and English alike, their allegiance to both crowns changing as often as their circumstances.

The Reiver's Return: In this atmospheric pen and ink drawing, a lone rider approaches Hollows tower, an Armstrong stronghold on the Esk. The rider is based on the Reiver monument in Galashiels and wears a back and breast, a burgonet and carries a Border lance. Note the high backed, sturdy saddle and the rolled blanket slung across his back. (P. Armstrong)

As the situation became increasingly intolerable, Wardens on both sides fought fire with fire, issuing a proclamation that 'All Englishmen and Scottishmen . . . are and shall be, free to rob, burn, spoil, slay, murder and destroy all and every such person and persons, their bodies, buildings, goods and cattle as do remain and shall inhabit the Debateable Land – without redress to be made for same'. Eventually, in an attempt to solve the problem, the two countries set up a Commission to divide the troublesome strip of land and after much wrangling, this was achieved by the erection of an earthen rampart known as the Scots Dyke. Although the extent of each country's responsibility was now defined, the area still retained its name and in spite of all the Wardens could do, the inhabitants, undeterred, remained 'ane great company of thieves and traitors'.

The author's model of a Border Reiver c. 1590. His combed burgonet is based on an example of German manufacture in the Kelvin Grove Museum, Glasgow and his torso is protected by a quilted jack. He wears long leather riding boots over Tudor hose and carries an eight-foot Border lance. In addition to his broadsword and dagger a small hand-wound crossbow known as a latch hangs from his saddle. (Border Miniatures, Keswick)

Wardens and Keepers

Appointed by their respective governments, Wardens were backed up by Deputies, Keepers, Captains, Land Sergeants and Troopers and were expected to meet with their opposite numbers at monthly Truce Days, the intention being to administer the Border Laws, 'keep the wild people of the three Marches in order' and dispense justice accordingly.

In an effort to ensure some degree of impartiality on the English Marches, it was the custom to confer the office of Warden on gentlemen from the southern counties of England, thus supposedly assuring the appointment of men who bore no obligation to the feuding factions over whom they were required to preside. Though a few good men undoubtedly did their best, many fell foul to temptation and soon became as corrupt and lawless as the folk with whom they were obliged to live. When a local man was appointed to the Wardenship, the results were invariably disastrous, as illustrated by the infamous career of Sir John Forster, a native Northumbrian who, in 1560, became Warden of the English Middle March. A regular subject of Border correspondence, he was the target of frequent accusations ranging from collusion with the Scots and neglect of duty, to using his office as a cloak for thieving and skulduggery, his accusers further adding that Sir John's catalogue of shortcomings 'would fill a large book'. Most of this was in fact true and his protestations of innocence are somewhat less than convincing.

It was evident, however, that by the 15th and 16th centuries the cost of war both at home and abroad had drained the resources of the Treasury and a Warden's salary was woefully inadequate, making it even more difficult to find the right man for the job. As a consequence, behaviour such as Forster's becomes understandable and any means by which a Warden could supplement his meagre income was fair game. 'Warden roades', official reprisal raids across the Border in order to punish habitual offenders, were often in reality large-scale, highly lucrative forays where large quantities of 'insight' (household goods), cattle, sheep, horses and weapons could be accumulated along the way. Prisoners, too, were often taken and subsequently ransomed.

As a rule, on the Scottish Border, the

First mentioned in 1242, Hermitage Castle – 'the Strength of Liddesdale' – was fortress to a succession of Border warlords, the most famous being James Hepburn, Earl of Bothwell, who in the mid 16th century strengthened 'Th' Armitage, meanyng to Kepe it by force'. In 1566, his lover and future bride, Mary Queen of Scots, rode from Jedburgh to Hermitage, crossing 50 miles of rough country in order to visit Bothwell after he had been badly wounded in a running skirmish with the notorious reiver, Little Jock Elliot. Eerie, gaunt and forbidding, Hermitage is steeped in legend and remains a fitting monument to the turbulent history of the Borders. (Courtesy of Historic Scotland) (P. Dougal)

Wardenship generally fell to the 'heidmen' of the powerful riding families, the idea being that Border lairds such as these could at least exercise some degree of restraint over their unruly kinfolk. That the theory was sound and, to some degree worked is evident in the following observation by Lord Scrope in 1586. Writing from the English West March to Queen Elizabeth's secretary of state, Sir Francis Walsingham, his anxiety regarding the loss of firm control in the opposing March is clearly apparent. 'I look to no justice from the opposite Border as I am told Maxwell has refused the Wardenry and every laird, gentleman and Borderer rides against the other. As the nights grow long and dark, I expect their accustomed insolencies against us will proceed afresh.' It was, however, obvious that the kind of justice meted out by such powerful figures as John, 8th Lord Maxwell or Buccleuch, was very often of a partisan and dubious nature. Not surprisingly, it was felt by some that they should not be allowed to hold such office at all, being native Borderers who were 'extraordinarilye addicted to parcialities' and 'favoured theire blood, tenantes and followers'.

Simply by carrying out his duties amongst such lawless and vengeful people, a Warden would make many enemies and the office was no guarantee of personal safety. In 1537, Roger Fenwick, Keeper of Tynedale, was murdered in Bellingham by 'three naughty persons' and at a Truce Day in 1585 Lord Russell was 'suddenly shott with a gonne and slain in the myddest of his owne men'.

Truce Days were held at recognised points along the Border, such as Windy Gyle, Foulden Rigg and Kershopefoot, and generally lasted from 'sonne to sonne'. Complaints and grievances, mainly concerned with the apprehension of murderers, 'broken men', stolen cattle, sheep and 'gear' (goods), were made in advance of the Truce Day, and the respective Wardens would endeavour to present the guilty parties for punishment, or make them pay some form of compensation to the injured party.

Justice was often swift and lethal, and death by beheading, hanging and drowning in 'murder holes', was commonplace along the Border. Truce Days also provided an occasion for the Border folk to meet one another, although the number from each side was supposedly limited to 1,000. Local pedlars and entertainers would attend and much drinking and carousing generally took place. Folk were expected to part company 'in all kindlie sort' but, not surprisingly,

these affairs often degenerated into mass brawls with loss of life on both sides, particularly so at the Reidswire in 1575.

A Warden also had other duties, including the maintenance of fortifications within his March, the setting of watches and beacons in order to apprehend raiders and the supervision of regular Courts and Sessions. When his March was raided, and the thieves took off into the night, the Warden was expected to fire the beacons, muster his followers and give chase. He was also required to pass on to central government any intelligence which might come his way concerning the opposite realm.

'Armed in plain hostility'

In 1286 Edward I, in pursuance of his ambitions for the complete annexation of Scotland, launched across the Border a series of devastatingly brutal incursions, plunging both countries into 300 years of warfare and earning him the sobriquet *Malleus Scotorum* – Hammer of the Scots. With the intention of totally demoralising and subjugating the Scots, his invading armies passed through the Borderland putting whole communities to the sword. Castles, villages, hill farms and hovels were burnt or destroyed, cattle and sheep stolen, crops devastated and the inhabitants slaughtered.

Inevitably the Scots retaliated in a similar fashion and invading armies were met with scorched earth policies, each outrage provoking a brutal reprisal. As this terrible war of attrition continued, both governments encouraged their Borderers to constantly harass their neighbours across the line with incessant raiding. Under Robert the Bruce, Scotland eventually had her day at Bannockburn in 1314 and to reinforce the point, his victorious armies systematically savaged the Northern Marches of England. The repeated blows by both sides were largely absorbed by the Borderland, turning it into a charred and impoverished wasteland and, as a consequence, by the beginning of the 16th century, the Border

A 'Steill Bonnett' of the Anglo-Scottish Borderland, this fine burgonet dates from 1570. The skull is raised from one piece of steel and then ground to shape, producing fine, glancing surfaces upon which a *sword blade can gain no purchase. This particular example is beautifully preserved and has a golden-brown patina from regular polishing with sheep fat. (Museum of Border Arms and Armour, Teviotdale)*

Marches were in a pitiful state. No man, woman, child, beast or building was safe from the marauding bands of riders who swept down from the hills to murder, burn and steal.

Caught up in a never ending cycle of violence, the Borderer quickly came to realise that due to the sudden and brutal nature of the conflict, the government who claimed his allegiance could provide him with neither justice nor protection and that his only strength and safety lay in his family, or clan. It was here, therefore, that his loyalty lay, and, living in what had virtually become a battlefield, it became unimportant to him which nation was in the ascendant. Survival became the most crucial element in his uncertain life and riding with his clan, he too joined in the grim business of raiding, or 'reiving' from equally desperate neighbours across the Border. Inevitably as time wore on these 'forays' were supplemented by raids nearer home on his own countrymen.

The Bishop of Carlisle, writing of the English Middle March in 1518, reported that 'there is more theft, more extortion by English thieves than there is by all the Scots in Scotland' adding indignantly that 'in Hexham every market day there is four score or a hundred strong thieves' openly loitering. Those who could not defend themselves or were unfortunate enough not to belong to one of the powerful Border families, or 'graynes', were subject to extortion and blackmail, paying money or crops in exchange for protection against raiders. Many folk had little to offer and suffered accordingly.

It is also worth mentioning that should a mutually attractive target present itself, raids were often undertaken in league with kindred spirits from across the Border. Help was also available in the furtherance of personal vendettas, such as the Maxwell–Johnstone feud on the Scottish side, as when the latter enlisted 'diverse Englishmen, treasonably brought within the realm, and armed in plain hostility'.

These cross-Border raiding alliances were com-

plex, shifting affairs and inevitably proved to be a constant source of frustration to the March Wardens. Marriage across the Border – though it could incur the death penalty – was commonplace and offered an unofficial kind of dual nationality. In a world of deadly feud, blackmail and murder, the advantages of being able to slip across the Border into the opposite realm when the forces of law and order were in hot pursuit, were obvious to miscreants on both sides of the line. As a harassed Border official, Thomas Musgrave, succinctly put it, 'They are people that will be Scottishe when they will and English at their pleasure.'

By and large, both Scots and English raiders conducted their business with an arrogant disregard for the forces of law and order, whose job it was to stop them. An indication of how confident they were is reflected in the desperation which is clearly evident in this account of repeated Scottish incursions into the English East March in 1590. 'In February last, 200 Liddesdale theives burned Myndrome, the barns, corn and cattle, carrying off goods worth £300 or £400. I have had no day of truce with the Scottish Warden since last October, which is one great cause of the theives boldness. These Liddesdale men are the most disordered in the Border – they come in great bands through Tevedall and the "marc"

A distinctive 'combed' morion of 1570. The whole helmet is raised from one piece of steel, including its high comb. This was, perhaps, one of the most difficult tasks for the armourer to perform and such examples were highly prized possessions. Apprentices were often required to raise such a testing piece in order to qualify as armourers. (Museum of Border Arms and Armour, Teviotdale)

[merse] into these East Marches and return with their booty, going the same way without resistance . . . Also, they dwell so far within their country from the East Marches that revenge by us is almost impossible.'

If authority seemed unable or unwilling to take direct action against such people, it is perhaps under-standable when one considers the following report. Written by Sir Robert Carey, an English Border officer of the 1590s, it is ominously instructive. 'This country has become almost slaves to the Scots and dare do nothing to displease them. If the country rise against them when they are stealing in England and either kill one by chance or take him "with the bloody hand" delivering him to the officer for execution and if they be foot lownes and men of no esteame amongst them, it may pass unrevenged, but if he is of a surname . . . or any they make accompt of, then he

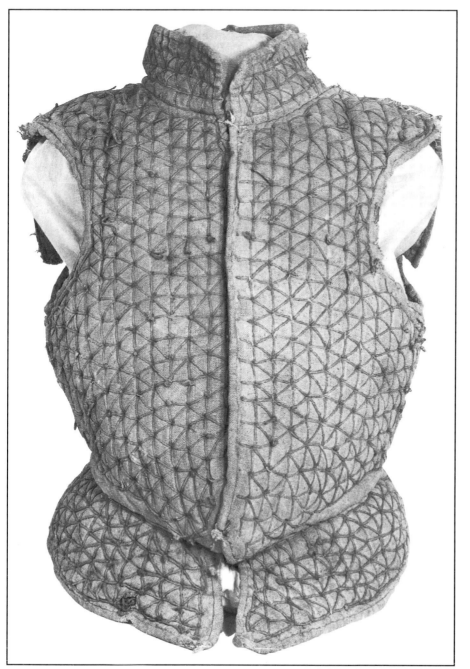

The common man's preferred alternative to plate armour, the ubiquitous 'jack' or 'jak of plaite' was flexible, highly protective and not too expensive to manufacture. Possibly originating in the North of England or Scotland the 'jak of plaite' found widespread use in Britain and is constantly referred to in Border musters of the 16th century. This well-preserved example is from Langlee in Roxburghshire and dates from the 1580s. (The Board of Trustees of the Royal Armouries)

This backsword, dated 1560, is an excellent example of the 'Skottish short sword' referred to in contemporary documents of the mid 16th century. With a blade measuring 31 in. it incorporates a full basket hilt of the type known as 'Irish'. This style actually originated in Scotland, but to the English, all Gaelic speaking Highlanders were classed as 'Irish'. (Museum of Border Arms and Armour, Teviotdale)

who killed or took him, is sure himself, and all his friends – especially those of his name – is like dearly to buy it, for they will have his life or two or three of his nearest kinsmen in revenge for their friends so killed or taken stealing here.'

That central government was well aware of this lamentable state of affairs is evident from the mass of correspondence they received from the March Wardens. Henry VIII, however, was content to keep his northern Border in a constant state of ferment, thus distracting the Scots and enabling him to pursue his military ambitions in Europe. This policy was clearly reflected in the Duke of Northumberland's assurance that he would 'let slip them of Tynedale and Redesdale for the annoyance of Scotland' and by Lord Dacre's intention to 'make a raid at least once a week while grass is on the ground'. As always the Scots responded with enthusiasm, were 'ever ryding' and generally managed to be 'most offensive to England'.

And so, by the middle of the 16th century, as life in the south of England was beginning to reflect a degree of stability and prosperity, the Anglo-Scottish Borderland was still locked in the grip of medieval warfare and had become a network of castles, towers, peles and strongly fortified farmhouses known as 'bastles'. Alongside them had evolved a formidable race of light horsemen, skilled in the art of raiding, scouting, ambush, feint and skirmish. Exasperated Border officials cursed them often as 'evell desposed people' who were 'inclined to wildness and disorder' and occasionally, with good reason, saluted them as being fine soldiers who were 'able with horse and harness', 'a military kind of men, nimble, wilie, and always in readiness for any service'.

'ARRAYED IN MOST WARLIKE MANNER'

Whether conscripted by the army in times of war as a 'pricker', serving his country as light horseman, skirmisher and scout, or in his role of raider, operating deep inside hostile territory and pitting his wits against the Warden's troopers, the dynamics which determined the reiver's success and survival were the same: stealth, surprise, cunning, boldness and, most importantly, speed. By carefully selecting his weapons, equipment and horse, he had developed the ability to harass the enemy and outstrip his pursuers, moving across both battlefield and hazardous terrain with alarming speed.

The Borderer was born into the saddle and placed great importance on his choice of mount. Needing a horse with the agility and stamina to carry him swiftly and safely across bog, moss and moorland, he chose the small sturdy 'hobbler' or hackney. Known in Scotland as a 'galloway' and in Northumberland as a 'nagg' or 'bog trotter', these shaggy little ponies, sure footed and reliable, were quite capable of transporting a man from Tynedale to Teviotdale and back in 24 hours. It would also seem that these beasts required little or no attention and were 'never tied up or dressed (groomed) but are turned immediately after the days march to pasture on the heath, or in the field'.

The reiver's hit-and-run tactics dictated that lightness and flexibility were of the essence and as a

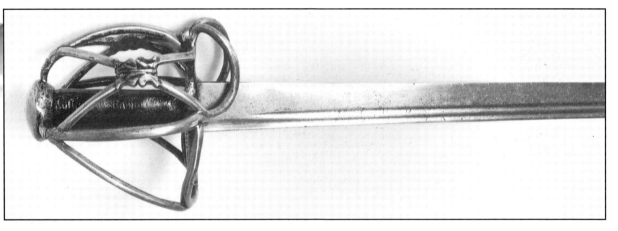

consequence, even in the early 16th century when suits of plate armour were still fashionable on the battlefield, he rarely encumbered himself with heavy defensive equipment that would slow him down. No doubt in times of national conflict, the wealthier Borderer may well have engaged the enemy in armour of quality, but the majority were poor men and much of their equipment would be handed down, stolen, captured or adapted to fit. As the 16th century wore on, and the use of firearms – 'gonnes', 'hackbutts' and 'daggs' – became more prevalent, the emphasis on speed and manoeuvrability became even more significant and the use of plate armour began to decrease accordingly, shrinking to back-and-breasts with the option of articulated thigh defences.

Most Borderers, rich and poor alike, preferred to protect themselves with a 'jack' or 'jak of plaite'. First mentioned in the late 14th century, the ubiquitous jack was relatively cheap to manufacture and it swiftly became the principal body defence of the common fighting man, retaining its popularity until the end of the 16th century. Usually sleeveless and occasionally worn over a shirt of mail, the jack was constructed from two or three layers of quilted cloth, twill or linen, between which were stitched small overlapping iron plates. Often cut from old armour and of crude appearance, these plates were between 2.8 and 3.9 cms square (1-1½ ins.). Each plate was pierced in the centre for the cord stitching, which formed a latticework pattern on the exterior of the garment. It extended from the neck to the upper thigh and fastened down the chest by means of hooks or thongs. The jack gave the wearer a combination of lightness and flexibility whilst retaining the ability to turn a sword cut as effectively as any armour. Jacks were usually faced with a dense, heavy material such as fustian, canvas or stout leather.

William Patten, an observer who accompanied Somerset's campaign into Scotland in 1547, describes the Scots at the Battle of Pinkie, as coming to the field 'all clad a lyke in Jackes covered in whyte leather, with doublets of the same or of fustian'. Being 'all clad a lyke' had its disadvantages. Patten ascribes the high mortality rate amongst the Scottish lairds at Pinkie to this 'vileness of port' and 'lack of brooch, ring, or garment of silk', meaning that few of them could be identified as worth the effort of capture for subsequent ransom.

Many Borderers wore chains of brass or pewter 'drawn four or five times along the thighs of their hosen and doublet sleeves [against] cutting' and every man had 'a great kercher [scarf] wrapped twice or thrice about his neck; not for cold, but [against] cutting'. Gauntlets of steel and leather were worn, some being of a similar construction to the jack, and covered in doeskin. Leg armour is rarely mentioned in Border musters of the 1500s, protection usually being afforded by stout, thigh-length, heel-less leather riding boots, worn with spurs. Small shields known as 'bucklers' were carried, as were studded, leather-covered targes, and Borderers serving in Ireland in the 1580s are shown carrying substantial round shields bearing the red cross of St George on a white field.

'Steill bonnetts'

In the early 1500s helmets ranged from a simple steel cap or 'skull' to the sallet, which though restricting peripheral vision , gave good protection to the upper part of the face and neck. By the middle of the 16th century, however, these helmets, though still in service, began to give way to the light open helmet known as the burgonet. Soundly constructed and combining a stylish, elegant appearance with a functional design, these 'steill bonnetts' offered maximum protection to the wearer without any loss of vision. Usually peaked, with protective cheek plates and a flared rim which protected the neck, the burgonet often incorporated a strengthening comb over the crown. Some fine examples, made in Germany and northern Italy, found their way into the Border country and most show evidence of a padded lining, usually of leather. Many of these helmets were 'blackened' or fitted with cloth or leather covers, to protect against inclement weather.

Equally fashionable by the 1580s and available in a variety of styles was the morion. In its most common form the helmet was known as a Spanish morion. Sitting low on the head, its tall shape and narrow rim earned it the nickname 'pikeman's pot'. Its use was widespread and it came in a basic munition grade for the common footsoldier but was also available in a lavishly decorated form for the wealthy. Similar, but lighter and with a wider, flared rim was the 'cabacette' morion, distinguishable by the curious rearward facing steel stalk which crowned it. The morion was perhaps at its most distinctive in its later 'combed' form. Often mistakenly called a Spanish morion it is instantly recognisable by its high comb and wide, sloping rim, which dips from front to rear in a sharp, downward curving arc. Occasionally issued with ear flaps, it was highly protective and like the rest of its family was available in varying degrees of quality and decoration.

Although Border Laws required all able-bodied men to appear at Muster Days with all the arms and armour at their disposal, it is extremely doubtful whether any Borderer would have been prepared to show his full hand to any kind of government official. Bearing this in mind, we are still fortunate that muster rolls from the 1500s have survived the passage of time, giving us an invaluable record of the Borderer's appearance. The lance, 'staff' or 'lang spear' was by far the commonest weapon available and many fighting men seem to have been furnished with 'lance, steel cap and jak of plaite'. Lances were used couched and ranged from 2.4 to 3.6 metres (8–12 feet) in length, the Borderer being very adept in their use. Swords are not as frequently mentioned as might be expected, but Patten informs us that the Scots at Pinkie were equipped with 'swords all notably broad and thin, of exceeding good temper and universally so made to slice that [he] never saw any so good'. Examples that have survived from the period are well made, usually with German blades and have good barred protection for the knuckles. Basket hilted broadswords predominated among the less wealthy near the end of the 16th century, while the nobility wore rapiers and parrying daggers. Dirks, home-made fighting knives, and long narrow daggers appear to have been carried by all and sundry, including the clergy.

Even though firearms were finding increasing favour in many quarters the longbow is frequently alluded to and the English Borderers, no doubt remembering past hammerings they had inflicted with it, seemed reluctant to give up its use. The Rev. William Harrison writing in 1588 berates the Englishman for not practising with his longbow, stating that 'Reiters' (German mercenaries) were 'deriding our archery' and 'turn up their tails and cry "Shoot English", and all because our strong shooting is decayed and laid in bed'. He goes on to point out that 'if some of our Englishmen now lived that served King Edward III . . . the breach of such a varlet [would] be nailed to his back with one arrow; and another feathered in his bowels before he should have turned about to see who shot the first'. The Borderers seemed to agree, for as late as 1580 there were still 1,100 bows and strings, with 4,900 arrows, being held in store at Newcastle, and in 1575, at the Raid of Reidswire the Tynedalers let fly with trusted bows and arrows. The Scots also used the bow, but not as significantly, or with such effect as the English and seemed to prefer the small light crossbow known as a latch.

The Scots Borderer, when fighting on foot, carried the 16 foot pike, the English still favouring the tried and trusted bill with its lethal spike, hook and heavy, single cutting edge. Also in use from the beginning of the 16th century was the 'Jeddart Staff'. Made by the armourers of Jedburgh this uniquely awesome weapon sported a slim 1.25 metre (4 feet) blade of steel, the lower half of which was set into a staff, thus providing the Borderer with a long cutting edge and a wicked spike for piercing. Long iron strips extended down the oak shaft to prevent the head of the weapon being lopped off and vamplates – iron shields – were fitted to protect the hands.

The last half of the 16th century saw the growing

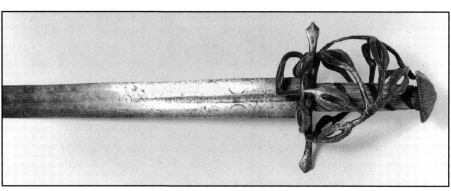

A German basket hilted broadsword dated 1570. Its blade, 32½ ins. long, bears an armourer's mark, two reversed 'sickle marks' and an orb and cross mark inlaid in copper. It sports broad quillons and exquisite guards in the 'schiavona' style. (Museum of Border Arms and Armour, Teviotdale)

use of hand-held firearms, mostly in the shape of the 'dagg', a heavy, single shot, wheel-lock pistol, and the 'caliver', a light wheel-lock carbine which could be used by cavalrymen. Most of these weapons were imported from Germany and, though tedious to reload and maintain, the wheel-lock mechanisms allowed them to be carried safely while primed. They could also be fired immediately, regardless of weather conditions. Large quantities of these 'gonnes' were available to garrison soldiers at Berwick and Newcastle, but many of them seem to have remained in storage and were allowed to fall into decay. Whether stolen or legitimately acquired, Borderers certainly carried these weapons, particularly the pistols, but such pieces were used with caution for some of them 'when they were shot in, broke and hurt divers mens hands'. Unless used at close range, these handguns were not particularly accurate and as they were dangerously slow to reload on the battlefield, it was customary to carry a pair. Commenting on the erratic marksmanship of his calivermen, a mercenary captain serving in the Scottish Lowlands advised that anyone who knew his men as well as he did 'would hardly choose to march before them!'

'With fyre and sworde'

Hardened by 300 years of constant turmoil and inured to suffering by the daily violence and feuding by which they lived, it is not surprising that the 'companies of wicked men' who rode out across the mosses and moorland, venturing life and limb in search of plunder, had, by the 16th century, honed the art of reiving to a wickedly fine edge. The following passage, penned by Bishop Leslie, in the 1570s, gives us a vivid description of the reiver going about his business.

'They sally out of their own Borders in the night in troops, through unfrequented byways and many intricate windings. All the daytime they refresh themselves and their horses in lurking places they have pitched upon before, till they arrive in the dark at those places they have a design upon. As soon as they have seized upon the booty, they in like manner, return home in the night through blind ways, fetching many a compass. The more skilful any captain is to pass through those wild deserts, crooked turnings, and deep precipices, in the thickest mists and darkness, his reputation is the greater and he is looked upon as a man of excellent head.'

Judging from the following catalogue of theft, burning, rustling and murder (which generally went unpunished) there appears to have been an abundance of such men in the Border Marches.

NOTE OF SPOILS IN MIDDLE MARCH – AUGUST 23, 1587
(From Sir Cuthbert Collingwood to Walsingham)

On 8th July, 4 men of E. Tevedale took out of Alnwick park within half a mile of Sir John Forster's house, 4 horses.

On 9th July, 12 of same took from Ditchburne, 40 beasts.

On 13th July, 30 of same, took at East Lilburne and Waperdon, hurting 5 men in peril of their lives in pursuit, 24 oxen and kyne and 60 sheep.

On 14th July, 4 of the same took from Ingram church, 4 'webbes of leed' (lead).

A robust, well-made example of a 'Spanish' morion – c. 1580, probably the most widely worn helmet of the 16th century. Raised from one piece of steel the rivets hold in place a canvas strip to which a lining of leather or padded cloth would have been attached. (Museum of Border Arms and Armour, Teviotdale)

On 15th July, 12 of same took out of Strangwood John Horssley's house, 120 sheep.

On 16th July, 40 of W. Tevedale took out of Byrkhouses in Redesdale, 40 oxen and kyne.

On 18th July, 300 of E Tevedale took out of Warton within 2 miles of Harbottle, and hurt 3 men, 30 oxen and kyne, 6 horses.

On same day, 6 men of same took out of Fadon, 80 sheep.

On 20th July, 20 of W Tevedale took from Horseley, besides 2 men hurt on defence, 30 kyne.

On 23rd July, 8 of E Tevedale took at Beanly, 100 sheep.

On St James's day, 20 of Liddesdale came in the day time to Haughton upon the water of Tyne, and broke and spoiled the house of Thomas Erington gentleman, to the value of 100*l.* in household stuff, and 30 kyne and oxen.

On 28th July, 20 of E. Tevedale came in the evening to Eslington, Sir Cuthbert Collingwood's dwelling house, and hurt 2 of his servants, and took 3 geldings.

On 7th August, the Laird of Buckclugh with 200 men, burned the Woodsyde at Riddesdale and murdered one John Dunne.

On 9th August, 160 of W. Tevedale burned Netherton with 2 miles of Harbottle and carried away 80 cattle.

On 11th August, 400 of E Tevedale took up Old Bewick, and carried away 500 oxen and kyne, 600 sheep, 30 horses and mares. On same night other 40

took away from Reveley, and burnt a house, 200 sheep, 30 kyne and oxen, 15 horses.

Sum Totals – 100 horses and mares, 1148 oxen and kyne, 1020 sheep besides 20 prisoners ransomed and many hurt in defence.

Reiving was a seasonal business, the prime time usually being from late August to February. Sir Robert Carey tells us that 'Border thieves will never lightly steal hard before Lammas [1st August] for fear of the assizes, but being once passed, they return to their former trade and unless in such yeares as they cannot ride upon the wastes by reason of stormes and snowes, the last moneths of the yeare are theyr chiefe time of stealing, for then are the nights longest, theyr horses hard at meate and will ride best, cattell strong and will drive furthest; after Candlemass [2nd February] the nightes grow shorter, all cattell grow weaker and, oates growing dearer, they feed their horses worst and quickly turn them to grass.'

'Outragious forradging'

Raids were carefully planned and as a rule the size and strength of the target would determine the number of men involved. Raiding parties could range from a dozen men on a swift moonlight foray, the

A popular helmet, the cabasset, or cabacette, was available in a variety of styles and sizes. This example dating from 1580, is raised from a single piece of steel and sports the usual, distinctive pear stalk terminal on its crown. It is said that the higher the helmet, the higher the rank, possibly making this one the property of an officer or a gentleman. (Museum of Border Arms and Armour, Teviotdale)

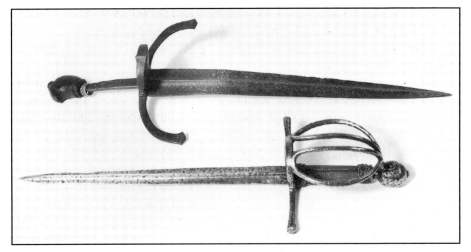

(Top) A rare example of a Lowland Scots left-hand dagger with bird's head pommel. Dating from the early 16th century, the only other example was allegedly taken from James IV's body by the Earl of Surrey after the Battle of Flodden Field 1513. (Bottom) A Lowland Scots dagger of 1590. This fine example has developed side bars and a side ring to match the early 'Irish' or basket hilted sword. (Museum of Border Arms and Armour, Teviotdale)

objective being the sacking of a single bastle and the lifting of a few beasts, to an example of 'outragious forradging', as in 1593 when a cut-throat army consisting of 'Dyverse Scottes to the number of two thousand or thereabouts . . . runne a forrowe [foray] within England and have taken and driven away out of Tyndall about nyne hundreth threescore and five kye and oxen and about a thousand sheep and goates, besides insight, clothes, gear and weapons'. These large, scale forays could last for two or three days, whilst the raiders, 'delighting in all mischief', sacked the surrounding countryside and generally behaved in a 'warlick mannor'. The resulting devastation impoverished whole valleys 'to the undoing of Her Majesty's subjects there', who, it might be added, were frequently left homeless, 'cutt in pieces' and 'extremely hurt and mangled'.

Ambitious raiders penetrated deeply on both sides of the Border, English reivers sacking villages on the outskirts of Edinburgh, whilst the Scots, crossing the Tyne, raided in the Bishopric of Durham and, on occasion, probed as far south as Yorkshire. It cannot be emphasised too strongly that by the 1550s these 'spoylings', both large and small scale, were taking place night after night with monotonous regularity, and honest local folk hardly seem to have had time to draw breath before English and Scottish 'theves' descended upon them with 'fyre and sworde'. The following comments, pertaining to the village of Corbridge in Tynedale, were no doubt representative of the plight of many similar communities elsewhere, which were 'very well inhabyted with men of good service and have very

good fermes and hable to kepe much cattell, . . . corn and hay, were yt not for the contynual robryes and incursions of the theves of Tyndall which so contynually assault them in the night'.

As a perpetrator of this kind of ruthless foraying, the Scottish laird, Walter Scott of Buccleuch, had few equals. A titled landowner who was aggressive, arrogant and brave, he has been immortalised in the Border Ballads as the 'Bold Buccleuch', whose daring rescue of Kinmont Willie Armstrong from Carlisle Castle in 1596 caused Lord Scrope so much embarrassment. Border Officer or Border reiver as it suited him, he could also be treacherous, a murderer without conscience and after the Union of the Scottish, and English Crowns in 1603, turned viciously on his own kind when it became politically expedient to do so.

Brought up on the Scottish Border, his regular involvement in countless raids, reprisals and deadly feuds made him a formidable opponent. In a complaint against him from the English West March in November 1588, we have a classic example of a well-planned raid, of the kind which characterised his exploits. 'Captain Steven Ellies and the surnames of the Rowtledges in Bewcastle, complain upon the said laird of Bucklughe, the laird of Chesame, the young laird of Whithawghe, and their accomplices to the number of 120 horsemen "arrayed with jackes, steil capps, speares, gunis, lancestaffes, and dagges, swordes and daggers" purposely mustered by Bucklughe, who broke the house of Wille Rowtledge, took 40 kye and oxen, 20 horse and meares, and also laid an ambush to slay the soldiers and others who should follow the fray, whereby they cruelly slew and murdered Mr Rowden, Nichell Tweddell, Jeffraye Nartbie and Edward Stainton, soldiers; maimed sundry others and drove 12 horses and meares, whereof they crave redress'. In addition to being perfectly executed, the incident combined all the elements essential to a successful foray: a carefully chosen target; trusted companions well armed and in sufficient numbers; the advantage of surprise; plus the good sense to anticipate pursuit and deal with it accordingly. Reiving was, however, a risky business and raiders did not always have it their own way.

'Hot Trod, hue and cry'

No matter how experienced, the reiver had many obstacles to overcome. Towns were generally secure and well defended and even small communities did not always give in easily, trading knock for knock, as witnessed by the behaviour of the inhabitants of Bywell in the Tyne valley. These 'handy craftsmen whose trade is all in yron worke for the horsemen and borderers of that country . . . making byttes, styrropes, bridles and such othere . . . are subject to the incursions of the theaves of Tyndale and compelled wynter and somer to bryng all their cattell and sheepe into the strete in the night season and watch both ends of the strete; and when th' enemy approachith, to raise hue and cry whereupon the town preparith for rescue of their goodes which is very populous by reason of their trade, and stoute and hardy by contynual practyse agenst th' enemy'.

Local watches were formed, and Bishop Ridley, best known as a Protestant martyr under Queen Mary, who was born in the tower of Willimoteswick, near Haltwhistle, recalled of the early 1500s, 'In Tynedale, when I was a boy, I have known my countrymen watch night and day in their harness . . . that is in their jackes and spears in their hands.' In 1587 Lord Henry Hundson, the March Warden,

gives us an encouraging example of what could be achieved when honest Borderers took arms against a party of Scottish raiders who 'returned thorrowe the West March meaning to take up two townes theare and carry awaye the goods. The contrie roase, reskewed the goods and chaste them into Scotland, kylled one of them, hurt another and took him prisoner and brought away 12 horsseys.'

Known 'theaves roades', passes and 'ingates' were patrolled by Wardens' troopers and often backed up by paid militia. Local officials were responsible for appointing 'setters and searchers' and as Ralph, Lord Eure advised Burghley, the Queen's chief minister, in 1597, 'The native countrymen are better at handling spears on horseback than the Yorkshire or Bishopric men, better prickers in a chase as knowing the mosses, more nimble on foot, and some keep "slewe dogges" [hounds] to serve the country, which the country could not pay for. Also divers of them live in the "Highe Streete" where the malefactors pass, not 4 or 5 miles out of Hexham, next the Waste, and few are landed or rich men and failing the pay, cannot keep horses.'

Bridges, which offered a quick passage home to fleeing raiders, were often chained against them, forcing the use of fords which were usually guarded day and night for precisely that reason. If it was known that marauders were riding, full watches or 'plumps' were mustered with perhaps twenty men replacing the normal two or three. In addition, both sides of the Border had a network of beacons which gave warning of approaching raiders. Controlled on the English side from Carlisle and from Home castle in Scotland, they were situated on towers and hillsides, and in 1570, an order from the Earl of Sussex warned that 'Every man that hath a castle or tower of stone shall, upon every fray raised in the night, give warning to the countrie by fire on the topps of the

This is a good example of the everyday fighting sword of the Border Marches. Found at Kershopefoot, a Warden meeting point in the Scottish Middle March, it has a 32½ ins. blade and features an 'Irish' basket hilt. (Museum of Border Arms and Armour, Teviotdale)

castle tower in such sort as he shall be directed from the warning castle, upon paine of 3s. 4d.' One beacon signalled raiders approaching, two warned they were approaching fast and four, that they rode in great strength.

Having negotiated the wastes, and sacked the bastle, tower or village, the reiver was never more vulnerable than when returning home from a foray. Often laden with booty and driving large numbers of cattle and sheep before him, he became conspicuous and dangerously slowed down. Writing to Burghley in 1596, Sir Robert Carey gives us a graphic description of the fate which often awaited just such an unfortunate band of raiders. 'This night being abroad with the twenty guarrison men allowed me a

watching, it was our good happe to mete with the Burnes, the principallest theves of Tyvidale, with goodes dryving before theme which thei had stollen. Wee kild twoe of theme furthright, tooke the third sore wounded before he would yeald, and the fourth, the night being darck, unhappelye scapte awaye. Before winter passes, I expect many such morning works if I continue here . . . and either weary them of night stealing, or they me of watching.'

An additional hazard to raiders was the ancient custom of 'Hot Trod'. Honoured under the Border Laws it allowed those who had been 'spoyled' to mount a pursuit within six days of the incident, cross the Border if necessary and to follow 'their lawful trod with hound and horn, with hue and cry and with all the accustomed manner of freshe pursuit for the recovery of their Goods spoiled'.

It was the duty of all neighbours between the ages of 16 and 60 whether receiving payment from the injured party or not, to join the Trod and 'follow the fray'. With its legality signalled by a piece of burning turf, held aloft on a spearpoint, the posse also had the right to recruit help from the first town it came to. Failure to comply could have serious consequences, for 'Whosoever hydes from the fray or turns again so long as the Beacon burns or the bell rings, shall be holden as Partakers to the enemies and used as Traitors, and fra thenceforth to be used as a fugitive and disobedient person.' Needless to say, raiders who were caught 'with the red hand' were dealt with on the spot, but if the thieves escaped and all else failed, the Borderer could always file a complaint with the Warden and hope for justice on the next Truce Day.

Many reivers must have ended their days in a midnight skirmish such as Carey's ambush described

German Reiters ('Ritters') armour of 1580. In addition to the Nuremburg guild mark the burgonet helmet bears the M.O. stamp of Martin Oham. The remainder of this 'black and white' armour is by Martin Rothschmeid of Nuremburg and is inscribed on the back plate with his initials. Usually armed with three wheel-lock pistols, an arquebus and a long thrusting sword known as an 'estoc', German reiters were employed by the English as mercenaries, acting as shock troops in support of regular forces. Many served against the Scots and it is likely that on occasion, quality armour such as this fell into the hands of Border reivers. (Museum of Border Arms and Armour, Teviotdale)

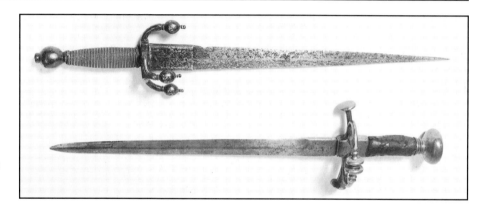

(Top) A left-handed parrying dagger with triple guard dating from 1580, and a similar piece (bottom) from Saxony, also dated to the late 16th century. In such a turbulent society most Borderers, including the clergy, carried such weapons as a matter of course. (Museum of Border Arms and Armour, Teviotdale)

above and many more spent their last moments on the gallows at Carlisle or Newcastle where they were 'condemmed and hanged, sometimes twenty or thirty'. In 1596, one such reiver, Geordie Burn, the night before he was executed, left behind him a unique confession which could perhaps stand as a fitting epitaph for them all. 'He voluntarily of himself said that he had lived long enough to do so many villainies as he had done and withal told us that he had lain with above forty men's wives, what in England, what in Scotland; and that he had killed seven Englishmen with his own hand, cruelly murdering them; that he had spent his whole time in whoring, drinking, stealing and taking deep revenge for slight offences.' Geordie was hung at first light.

'STRENGHES' AND 'BASTELLS'

As a direct response to the constant threat of attack by marauders, two distinct types of fortified dwelling appeared in the Border country: the tower house and the bastle. Large numbers were erected across the Borderland and it was said that 'not a man amongst them of the better sort hath not his little tower or pile'. The tower house was the home of the Border lord, whilst the bastle provided a simpler but secure refuge for the less wealthy gentleman or prosperous farmer. Stark, functional and immensely strong, these bastles are unique in the British Isles, the vast majority being found within 20 miles of the Borderline. An important factor influencing this location

were English Acts of Parliament of 1555 and 1584 which dictated that all 'fortalices', castles and towers within that distance were to be put in good order for defence and that all open ground was to be enclosed by quickset hedges and ditches in order to deter and hinder raiders.

The origins of such buildings lay in crude dwellings with walls of turf and clay which were usually reinforced with wooden stakes. Bishop Leslie observed that the Scots built 'towers of earth which can not be burnt, nor without great force of men of war, down can be cast', and even as late as the mid 16th century many poor people relied on such humble dwellings for shelter and protection. Relatively quick and easy to re-erect if destroyed and usually enclosed by a defensive palisade of wooden stakes or 'pales', these dwellings gradually gave way to the type of strong house or 'strenghe' described by Ralph Ellerker and Robert Bowes who surveyed Border defences for Henry VIII. They reported that the headmen of North Tynedale had 'very strong houses whereof for the most part the utter [outer] syddes or walls be made of greatt sware [square] oke trees strongly bounde and joyned together with greatt tenors of the same so thycke mortressed [morticed] that yt wylbe very hard without greatt force and laboure to break or cast down any of the said houses, the tymber as well of the said walls, as roofs, be so great and covered most part with turves and earth that they will not easyly burne or set on fyre'. Sounding remarkably similar to the frontier cabins which sprang up across North America in the 18th century, these primitive but highly defensible buildings were, however, already being superseded by the Border tower house.

Built of stone and mortar, the tower house was

generally enclosed by a defensive stone wall or 'barmkin' which replaced the earlier palisade. (The term 'pale' or 'pele' lingered on however, and is still used haphazardly when referring to Border towers.) Built for the safekeeping of cattle and sheep in times of trouble, the barmkin was usually between 5 and 6 metres (15–18 feet) high and a metre (3 feet) thick. Apart from the tower, it often enclosed a cluster of clay and wood dwellings belonging to the Lord's retainers and occasionally, even a chapel. The tower itself was generally of a rectangular shape measuring approximately 10×13 metres (30×40 feet) and rose to between 13–20 metres (40–60 feet) high. Constructed with massive corner stones and walls averaging between 1.5–3 metres (5–10 feet) thick it was immensely strong for its relatively small size. Usually towers took the form of a barrel vaulted basement, over which were two floors providing living accommodation. These were crowned by a steeply pitched roof, tiled with stone slabs and surrounded by a narrow gangway which was enclosed by a parapet. Usually crenellated, this allowed defenders a degree of protection while they hurled an interesting variety of objects down at attackers. Many roof areas also incorporated a stone lookout's seat, sometimes thoughtfully placed against the warm chimney breast in deference to cold Border nights. Alongside it would be fixed an iron fire-pan or brazier. Filled with

a mixture of pine roots and peat it would be fired on the approach of marauders. In the event of such a raid, the lord and his retainers, having secured their sheep and cattle within the barmkin, would retire to the tower. Milking cattle and horses would be led into the barrel vaulted basement, the small sturdy door being locked fast behind them.

Ventilation was provided by very narrow slits and 'shot holes' which were pierced high in the basement walls, the only internal access being via a 1 metre (3 feet) square trapdoor in the ceiling. This led to the first floor which provided accommodation for the inhabitants. Unless relieved by torchlight most rooms must have been dark and gloomy, for the emphasis was on total security and windows were few and narrow, with wooden shutters to keep out the harsh Border weather. Some windows, however, were bowed out to provide window seats and rudimentary cupboards were formed by recesses in the walls. One wall invariably featured a huge, open fireplace, its chimney tapering as it rose towards the roof. Floors were strewn with moor grass, heather and herbs, such as thyme and rosemary, and any furniture would be sparse, robust and practical. Chairs were a luxury, 'crackets' and 'lang settles' (low benches) being more common.

The second floor, which was supported on oak beams, led to the roof and could be used for sleeping or storage. As a rule, this floor would also house the garderobe, or toilet. Under normal circumstances access to the tower was via two doors at ground level, the first being of stout, studded oak, the second of interlaced iron bars, known as a 'yett'. The upper floors were reached by a narrow, spiral or 'newel' staircase, which was usually set within the thickness of the wall, and turned upwards in a clockwise direction, thus giving freedom of movement to a right-handed defender's sword arm used against an attacker trying to climb up. As a further hazard to intruders, these staircases occasionally featured a 'trip step', which, being much steeper than its fellows, could prove fatal to an unwary attacker absorbed in the business of close quarter combat in near darkness. If the attackers did manage to break

An engraving by Jost Amman dated 1584 depicting two well-armed German 'reiters'. Note the heavy arquebus and three wheel-lock pistols carried *by the rider on the right. In times of national conflict, wealthier Borderers may have been similarly attired.*

through the oak door and yett, these staircases could be blocked by furniture and boulders, which were held in readiness on each floor.

If the worst came to the worst, and, due to the approach of a large hostile force, the tower had to be abandoned, it would be emptied of valuables and then stuffed full of smouldering peat, making its outright destruction by gunpowder an extremely risky enterprise but allowing the rightful owners to return to an intact shell once the invaders had left. Rugged and forbidding in aspect, these towers must have seemed a daunting prospect to reiving bands, but they could be taken. The simplest way was to bombard them into submission, but Border terrain did not lend itself to the transportation of cumbersome pieces of artillery. (Most ordnance was in government hands anyway and was held largely for defence, in centres such as Carlisle, Berwick and Newcastle.) One tried and tested way was 'scumfishing', which involved hacking through the tower doors and heaping sodden straw into the doorway and against the walls. This was then fired and the defenders could be smoked out. Sometimes brute force prevailed, as when Buccleuch 'coming to the stone house of Banckheade-upon-Esk forcibly burst and burnt the door and the irone yeat, taking prisoners and household stuff'. Robert Carey favoured scaling ladders, by which his men were able 'to get to the top of the tower and to uncover the roof; and then some twenty of them to fall down together and by that means to win the tower'. Risky to say the least! The best method, perhaps, was by stealth and surprise, as illustrated by this 1547 account of the taking of Lochwood tower, a Johnstone stronghold near Moffat.

'We came thereabout an hour before day and the greater part of us lay without the barnekin; but about a dozen of the men got over the barnekin wall and stole close into the house within the barnekin and took the wenches and kept them secure in the house till daylight. And at sun-rising, two men and a woman being in the tower, one of the men rising in his shirt went to the tower head, and seeing nothing stir about, he called on the wench that lay in the tower and bade her rise and open the tower door and call up them that lay beneath. She so doing and opening the iron door and a wood door without it. Our men within the barnekin broke a little too soon

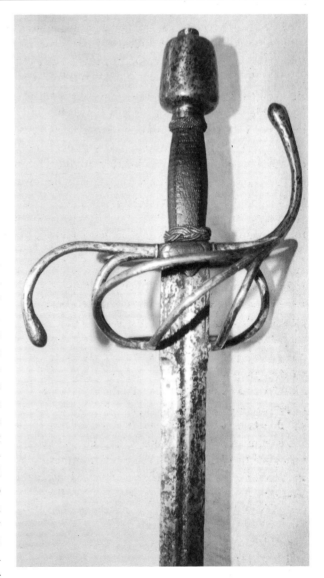

This elegant rapier, reputedly found in a wall recess in a public house in Cumbria, has a blade 36½ ins. long and features an elaborate pattern of twisted bars affording good protection to the hand. In the Borders it became common near the end of the 16th century to hide valuable weapons when their use became prohibited to ordinary citizens. (Museum of Border Arms and Armour, Teviotdale)

to the door, for the wench, perceiving them, leaped back into the tower and had gotten almost the wood door to, but one got hold of it that she could not get it close to; so the skirmish rose, and we over the barnekin and broke open the wood door and she being troubled with the wood door left the iron door open and so we entered and won Lochwood.'

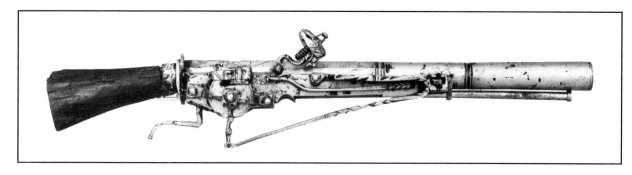

The last half of the 16th century saw the increased use of the hand-held firearm which found its most efficient and convenient form in the wheel-lock pistol. Its name is derived from the serrated wheel which, when the trigger is pressed, rotates against a shard of iron pyrites held clamped in 'dog' jaws, producing sparks which in turn ignite the priming powder. This rotation is powered by a strong spring held inside the lock plate which pulls a chain that winds round the wheel spindle. This spindle is square ended and protrudes through the lock plate, thus enabling the mechanism to be wound up with a long key. (The Board of Trustees of the Royal Armouries)

The 'bastell house'

The humbler option available to the wealthier farmer was the defensible farmhouse known as a bastle or 'bastell house' (from the French *bastille*: a fortified place). A massively strong, two-storey building with walls averaging over one metre (four feet) thick, its roof was steeply pitched and covered with stone slabs. Rectangular in shape and usually measuring between 10–13 metres (30–40 feet) by 6–8 metres (20–24 feet), the majority incorporated a basement which provided shelter for livestock. The basement was usually barrel-vaulted but some bastles supported their upper floors on huge, roughly cut oak beams. Accommodating the Borderer and his family, the upper floor generally boasted a fireplace and two or three small, narrow windows, all set well above ground level. Cattle, sheep or horses were driven into the basement via a small, solid door which would then be bolted from the inside, a small trapdoor in the ceiling giving access to the living quarters above. External access to the bastle was gained by climbing a removable wooden ladder which led to a stout, heavily bolted door, pitched high up in the bastle wall. Once the ladder was pulled up and the door bolted, the folk inside were as safe as anyone could be in such troubled times. For greater safety, bastles were often found in clusters, as at the village of Lessudden on the Scottish Border, where there were no fewer than 16. Each one was strategically placed in order to allow a murderous crossfire with dagg and bow, making an attempt on any single dwelling a hazardous undertaking. Many bastles which have survived have done so because they are still used as farm buildings and most now have external stone steps leading to the door, a feature introduced in later, more peaceful times.

'SPEARS, NORTHERN ON HORSEBACK'

Though Borderers were frequently castigated in peacetime for their unruly behaviour and warlike disposition, it was these very characteristics which made them so eagerly sought after by their national armies in times of war. Recruited into the English king's army as 'Bands of Northern Horsemen' or 'Border Horse', their commanders were quick to point out that 'a ruder and more lawless crew there needs not be' but also acknowledged that they were 'skilful, wary, experienced men' 'and if well tutored, . . . might do good service'. By 1546, the English army could boast 2,500 of them and it was soon noted that 'The most remarkable of the mounted men in Henry VIII's army were the Northern Horsemen, who, called into being by the eternal forays of the Scottish Border, were light cavalry, probably the very best in Europe.'

Under the control of a Captain General, Bands were comprised of Companies numbering 100 men, these being led by Captains, who were usually recruited from Border 'heidmen', thus ensuring loyalty

'Running a Foray', 1585
1: Border 'heidman'
2: Border Reiver
3: Border heidman's son
4: 'Foot lowne'

A

Flodden Field, 1513
1: Sir Edmund Howard
2, 3: Highland Scots
4, 5: Lowland Scots
6: The Bastard Heron

B

Solway Moss, 1542
1, 3: Mounted 'prickers'
2: Lowland Scots

C

'The Hot Trod', 1590's
1: March Warden
2: Trooper
3: Border rider

D

'A Day of Truce', 1590's
1: English March Warden
2: Scottish March Warden
3: 'Clark'
4: Border 'heidman'

E

F

3

1

2

Ireland, 1576
1: Border horseman
2: Galloglass
3: Kern

The Rescue of Kinmont Willie, 1596
1: Buccleuch
2: Kinmont Willie
3: Red Rowan
4, 5: Border Reivers

Moss Troopers, 1603
1, 2: Mounted moss troopers
3: Dismounted moss trooper

H

and a familiarity of command. Each Captain had under him a Petty-Captain and usually a trumpeter or standard bearer. There does not seem to have been a standard uniform, though a rather ambitious ordinance of 1540 required that 'Unladen gentlemen and yeomen have jacks of plate, halbriks, splints, sallet or steel bonnet, with pesanor gorget, and all to wear swords.' The Bishop of Durham, perhaps more realistically, expected a Border Horseman to wear a 'steel cap, coat of plate, boots, spurres, a skottish short sword and a dagger; a horsemans staffe and a case of pistolls', being much how he would appear whilst engaged on raid or foray. Most Borderers, whilst on national service, wore their country's colours in the shape of small crosses, red for England and blue for Scotland, of which we shall hear more later. By the mid 1500s the daily rate of pay for a 'Foot loone' (levied Border foot) was sixpence, a cavalryman eight pence, a petty captain two shillings and a captain four shillings. In order to supplement their income whilst on campaign, Borderers habitually kept an eye open for ransom, and were 'given much as they say, to the spoil' – often, as we shall see, to the peril of their fellow soldiers.

Recruited as light horsemen, 'prickers' or 'chasing staves', their role in the war machine was basically an extension of their daily activities on the Border Marches. Exploiting their own peculiar skills, they scouted for the army, ambushed the enemy's patrols, rustled his livestock, stole his supplies and provisions, plundered his towns and villages, and, when he was defeated and in full retreat, harassed and hunted down the remnants of his army.

In 1544, a large English force and attendant fleet, under the command of the Earl of Hertford, invaded the east coast of Scotland, sacking the towns of Leith and Dunbar, 'putting man, woman and child to fire and the sword' and capturing the Scottish capital, Edinburgh. Whilst the army was engaged in burning the city, they were joined by '400 light horsemen from the Borders, by the King's Majesty's appointment; who, after their coming did such exploits in riding and devastating the country, that within seven miles every way of Edinburgh, they left neither pele, village or house standing unburnt, nor stacks of corn; besides great numbers of cattle, which they brought daily in to the army and met also with much good stuff which the inhabitants of Edinburgh had for the safety of the same, conveyed out of the town'. Seasoned campaigners, they were involved in many a 'sharp onset' and traded 'hard knocks' with the enemy. Henry VIII regarded them as a *corps d'élite*, and when a London merchant snubbed him, the wretched man was assigned to the Border Horse, in order that he might taste 'the sharp discipline militair of the northern wars'.

Many Borderers served unofficial apprenticeships in the wars which raged across what are now the Low Countries and there are frequent references in Border papers to men serving as mercenaries in Holland, Flanders and in the 'Belgic' wars. This kind of military experience made their recruitment even more attractive, and in 1597 when Ralph Mansfield, the Keeper of Redesdale, was accused of enlisting George Hall of Birdhope – 'a notorious thief and murderer' in his Border patrol, he indignantly justified his actions by pointing out that Hall had been allowed to settle in Redesdale in recognition of his 'martial experience in the Netherlands'.

When, in 1544, Henry VIII ordered the recruitment of additional Border Horse for service in his French campaigns, two companies of 'picked and chosen men' from Tynedale and Redesdale were despatched to Montreuil where they joined the rest of the army under the Duke of Norfolk. Whilst in France they acquitted themselves well, skirmishing successfully against French scouts, cutting off enemy units, taking prisoners for interrogation and reporting on enemy movements and morale. It would seem Scottish prickers served in France also, but with the French, some of their number being observed escorting the defeated English out of Calais in 1568.

Border Horse also served in Ireland, particularly when the rebellions of O'Neill and Tyrone were in full swing. The English suffered many setbacks, and the Borderers were caught up in a ruthless war of attrition, facing an enemy as elusive and unorthodox as themselves. The Irish, fighting on their home ground, generally confined themselves to 'skirmishing in passes, bogs, woods and in all places [to their] advantage. And they hold it no dishonour to run away; for the last sconce and castle for their security is their feet'. To the Borderer, far from home and often poorly supplied, it must have all seemed depressingly familiar. Nevertheless, from what we are told, he could certainly hold his own against the light

Irish cavalry, whose main disadvantage it would seem was their practice of riding without stirrups. This, combined with a shallow, quilted saddle, invariably resulted in their being unhorsed when they clashed with their English counterparts, who 'having deep war saddles and using pistols as well as spears and swords – many of them having corselets [mail shirts] and like defensive arms, and being bold and strong for encounters and long marches, and of greater stature than the Irish, must needs have great advantage over [them]'. In 1540, it was pointed out that a hundred 'English spears, Northern on horseback' combined with a like amount of hackbutters and longbowmen would be a much more appropriate force than a thousand regular troops who were garrisoned in Ireland at that time. It should also be borne in mind that little mercy was shown by either side and the odds against survival were such that service in the Irish wars was often prescribed as a form of punishment. As no doubt was the intention, many Borderers never returned home.

'Able defenders of the realm' they may have been when it suited them, but as one might expect, there was a darker, far less commendable side to their behaviour. Never losing sight of their personal priorities they frequently left themselves open to accusations of murder, desertion, treason and theft. William Patten had the opportunity to observe them first hand whilst engaged on the Pinkie campaign and though he acknowledges their effectiveness as scouts and skirmishers on the march northwards, he clearly distrusts them.

Berating them for 'intolerable disorder and abuse' in camp, he goes on to criticise them for an obvious reluctance to allow national differences to interfere with their cross Border alliances, and clearly suspects them of collusion. He also hints at their transient loyalties and, if the need arose, implies how quickly they could switch their national allegiance from one side to the other. Speaking plainly, after the Battle of Pinkie, Patten ventures the following: 'Another manner they have among them is of wearing handkerchers rolled about their arms, and letters broidered upon their caps. They said themselves, the use thereof was that each of them might know his fellow, and thereby the sooner assemble, or in need to aid one another, and such like respects. Howbeit, there were of the army among us some suspicious men that thought they used them for collusion; and rather because they might be known to the enemy as the enemy are known to them, for they have their marks too, and so, in conflict, either each to spare the other, or gently each to take the other. Indeed men have been moved the rather to think so, because some of their crosses [the badge of the English army, a red cross on a white background] were so narrow and so

'*Auld Wat of Harden*' by Tom Scott RSA. Whilst beautifully evoking the Border landscape, Scott's paintings invariably tend to over-romanticise the Border reiver. Walter Scott of Harden, or 'Auld Wat', shown here in the heroic mould, was actually a notorious ruffian who plundered extensively on both sides of the Border. Being a veteran reiver, it is unlikely he would ever have overloaded himself with so much armour. His companions, however, mounted on sturdy 'galloways' and wearing 'steil caps' and back and breasts, look 'nimble' enough. Note the hound or 'slewe dogg' bottom left. (Mainhill Gallery, Ancrum)

singly [slightly] set on, that a puff of wind might have blown them from their breasts: and that they were found right often, talking with the Scottish prickers within less than their gads [spears] length asunder; and when they perceived they had been spied, they have begun to run at one another, but so apparently perlassent [in a make believe manner] that they strike few strokes but by assent and appointment. I heard some men say it did much augment their suspicion that way, because at the battle they saw these prickers so badly demean themselves, more intending the taking of prisoners than the surety of victory; for while other men fought they fell to their prey; that as there were few of them but brought home his prisoner, so were there many that had six or seven . . . our prickers, if their faults had been fewer, their infamy had been less.'

Flodden Field

Similar aspersions were cast on the conduct of Borderers on both sides after the Battle of Flodden Field in 1513, when the Bishop of Durham denounced the English Borderers as being 'falser than the Scots and have done more harm at this tyme to our folks than the Scots did. I would all the horsemen in the Borders were in France [with Henry VIII] for there should they do much good, whereas here they do non, but much harm; for they never lighted from their horses, but when the battle joined, they fell to rifling and robbing as well on our side as for the Scots, and have taken much goods besides horses and catell. And over that they took prisoners of ours and delivered them to the Scots, so that our folks as much fear them as they do the Scots.'

No doubt the Bishop was well informed, but it is worth measuring his comments against the Borderers' performance at Flodden on the previous day. The battle had commenced with an artillery duel, and whilst the Scots, drawn up on the ridge of Branxton Hill, were unable to depress their guns to a point where they could inflict casualties, the English gunners, shooting uphill, had no such problems and began to pulverise the motionless Scottish ranks above them. James IV's left flank, made up of Border pikes under Lord Home, and Gordons under Huntly, unable to endure the cannonade any longer, broke ranks and charged down Branxton Hill towards the English right wing, commanded by Edmund

Massively strong and in a fine state of preservation, this bastle-house at Gatehouse in Tarset is unusual in that its upper floor is supported by massive oak beams instead of the usual barrel vaulted ceiling. The external stone steps are a feature added in less troubled times. (Courtesy of Miss Maddison)

Howard. Outnumbered three to one, and totally unnerved by the approach of Home's massed array of pikes, the vast majority of Howard's division, men from Cheshire, Lancashire and Yorkshire, panicked and ran. Some men, including Howard, stood their ground and though now outnumbered by twenty to one, put up a desperate resistance. Assailed by pikes and the great, double-handed claymores of the Gordons, they began to go down, one by one until only a handful remained.

With his standard bearer dead and his standard captured, Howard was three times attacked and knocked to the ground by Home's Borderers, who, with an eye to ransom, almost had him taken, but each time, Howard managed to regain his feet, lashing out at those who came within range. Then, just as the Scots were about to rush him for the last time, 1,500 of Lord Dacre's English Border Lances crashed into the Scottish flank and a vicious melée ensued. Whilst the main body of Dacre's riders took on Home's pikemen, a small, hand-picked band of mounted Border ruffians, led by the recently outlawed Bastard John Heron, hacked their way through the Scots ranks and came to the rescue of the intrepid Howard. Taking him along with them, Heron's reivers 'making even work before them', continued to cut a bloody pathway through Home's pikemen, heading towards the main body of the English army.

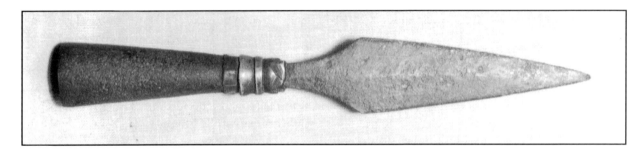

Whilst doing so they were confronted by a party of Scots led by Sir Davy Home, and it was Howard who personally cut the young laird down.

Meanwhile, the main forces of Dacre and Home were still locked together in combat and James IV, perhaps in the mistaken belief that the English army was beginning to disintegrate, chose this moment to abdicate his role as commander. Taking up a pike and joining the front rank of his own division, he led his magnificent army down the rain-soaked hill towards the waiting ranks of English billmen.

Just before the two armies met, Dacre and Home's forces disengaged and drew apart, Dacre returning to the gap left by Howard's fleeing contingent and Home withdrawing to his original position on Branxton Hill. Watching each other cautiously, neither force took any further part in the battle. Being Borderers, Home and Dacre were later accused of limiting their casualties by means of a tacit agreement, and though they both hotly denied it, few believed them. Dacre had lost 160 men to pike, bow and claymore, but he and his Border Lances had broken up the initial, and perhaps most dangerous Scottish onslaught. Holding his ground, he considered his duty done. Home, having successfully bloodied the English, and in the process lost a number of close relatives, Border lairds and four Gordon chieftains, had much the same point of view.

As daylight faded and the battle below him raged on, Home watched the English billmen carve ever widening bloody gaps in the Scottish ranks. When it became increasingly obvious that 'all was defeat', and he was pressed to go to the aid of his doomed King, Home shrewdly remarked that 'He does well that does for himself', adding that 'We have fought our vanguard already, let others do as well as we.'

Flodden was the worst blow Scotland had ever suffered. Her King and 10,000 of his men lay dead on the battlefield and the country lay open to invasion. Though Home was forever criticised for his inactivity that day, he was probably aware that English incursions would surely follow the victory and that he and his Borderers would be the only defence the Scottish Lowlands would have. Being a Borderer he made a practical decision and stood by it.

Solway Moss

Perhaps the English Border pricker had his finest hour at Solway Moss in the Western Marches on a November morning in 1542. By August of that year, both English and Scottish Borderers were being incited by their respective governments to cause as much mischief as possible, both sides fully realising that due to a series of snubs and long-running grievances, war was becoming inevitable. The Scottish reivers had responded with their usual enthusiasm and in reply, the Warden of the English East March, Robert Bowes, launched a massive reprisal raid, devastating Teviotdale and sending out smaller forays to savage the surrounding countryside. Whilst returning with its booty and livestock, the whole force was ambushed at Haddon Rig, by a small Scottish army under the Earl of Huntly. The English force included a contingent from Tynedale and Redesdale who, quickly sizing up the situation, deserted Bowes, and driving the stolen livestock before them, vanished into the hills. The remaining English were badly mauled and sent packing. For Henry VIII it was the final straw and he decided to settle the matter by force of arms. In October 1542, an English army of 20,000 Northern levies crossed the Scottish Border.

Kelso and Roxburgh were burnt and Teviotdale once again felt the weight of the sword. The English, however, were short of supplies and after a week of destruction, they returned to Berwick-upon-Tweed.

The Scots King James V had also raised an army of sorts, but on hearing the English had withdrawn, his nobles, who had little faith in their King, were reluctant to retaliate. Though the army was dis-banded, James doggedly gathered another force some 15–18,000 strong and while his adversary rested at Berwick, the new army marched south-west from Edinburgh and headed towards the English West March, Carlisle and Cumbria. Having set everything in motion, James decided to wait at Lochmaben, while his army rolled towards the Border under the temporary command of Oliver Sinclair. Regarded by

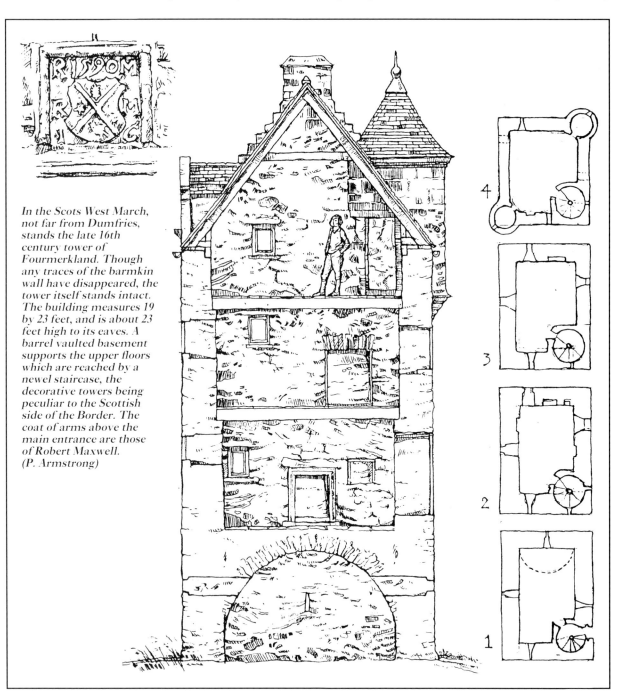

In the Scots West March, not far from Dumfries, stands the late 16th century tower of Fourmerkland. Though any traces of the barmkin wall have disappeared, the tower itself stands intact. The building measures 19 by 23 feet, and is about 23 feet high to its eaves. A barrel vaulted basement supports the upper floors which are reached by a newel staircase, the decorative towers being peculiar to the Scottish side of the Border. The coat of arms above the main entrance are those of Robert Maxwell. (P. Armstrong)

the other Scottish commanders as the 'King's hated favourite', the hostility and dissension his appointment caused would prove to be calamitous to the Scottish enterprise.

With the English army massed on the east coast, the only obstacle to the Scots advance was the garrison at Carlisle. On learning of the approaching invasion, their commander Thomas Wharton, Deputy Warden of the English West March, set about mobilising his 3,000 men. Learning he was outnumbered five to one, Wharton, Border veteran that he was, still decided to confront the enemy and inflict as much damage on them as he possibly could. By 24 November, dark plumes of smoke hung over the horizon as the Scottish army burnt their way across the Debateable Land, forcing the predatory Grahams into the surrounding hills. Wharton, watching from the vantage point of Arthuret Heights with his Cumbrian prickers, watched the main strength of the Scottish army advance towards the River Esk.

As the huge army began to ford the river, Wharton, with a skirmisher's eye, noticed how the Scots ranks were hemmed in by the banks of the river and how they would be unable to manoeuvre because of the surrounding marshland known as the Solway Moss. Realising he might never have a better opportunity, he deployed between seven and eight hundred of his prickers to maul the Scottish right flank.

As news of the bewildering and unexpected attacks reached Sinclair and the Scottish commanders, a dispute ensued amongst them as to what to do and confusion began to take hold of their army on the Esk ford. Sensing the growing panic they were causing, Wharton's prickers increased the ferocity of their attacks, hacking and slashing with broadsword and lance and discharging daggs and calivers into the Scots at point-blank range. Men crashed into one another, desperate to escape the vicious onslaught and Wharton, to his disbelief, watched the massive Scottish column begin to buckle and disintegrate. Men were trampled underfoot and many drowned.

Discarding their standards, cannon and handguns the Scots began a disorderly retreat. Amongst the 1,200 prisoners taken for ransom were numerous Lords, Barons and Earls and the unfortunate Oliver Sinclair. The retreat became a rout and, as the fugitive army fled back into Scotland across the Debateable Land, the recently dispossessed Grahams were waiting for them. Other Scottish Borderers, particularly those of Liddesdale, plundered the shattered army mercilessly making pursuit by the English unnecessary. Wharton's victory was complete. Using no more than 7–800 Border horsemen, he had smashed and routed a powerful Scottish army of between 15,000 and 18,000 men. His own casualties did not even reach double figures!

'TO CHASTISE THOSE BORDERS': 1603

In the last years of Queen Elizabeth's reign, lawlessness and raiding on the Border escalated to a point where, in desperation, a proposal was put forward to restore and rebuild the 'Pictish' or Roman Wall. Heavily fortified and costing in the region of £30,000, the reconditioned Wall would incorporate 'skonses' (castles) a mile apart, each of which would require 'a separate siege by an invading army', and would hopefully deter any further 'incurtyons or invacyons' by the Scots. Furthermore, it was cynically pointed out that the Wall and its fortified 'skonses' would also enable an English regular force to invade Scotland at any time! Though the idea was never actually taken up, the fact that such an enterprise was even proposed illustrates just how appalling conditions were becoming even when the two countries were supposedly at peace. The degree to which law and order had actually broken down was graphically underlined by Buccleuch's successful foray on Carlisle Castle in 1596, when he and a party of Armstrongs, Elliots and assorted Border ruffians broke loose the notorious reiver, Kinmont Willie Armstrong. Though the incident caused a political furore on both sides of the Border, Buccleuch justified his action by pointing out that Kinmont Willie had been taken prisoner by the English whilst attending a Truce Day, in blatant disregard of Border Law. Whilst this was true enough, it is easy to understand how a frustrated Warden like Scrope could not resist the temptation to arrest such an arrant freebooter, when all the legal means at his disposal had failed.

In keeping with the tenor of the times, a tradition

A Pringle stronghold, Smailholm tower stands in splendid isolation on a rocky knoll six miles west of Kelso. Dominating the surrounding landscape, it retains fragments of its barmkin wall and remains much as it would have looked in the 16th century. Smailholm was once owned by Sir Walter Scott's family, and no doubt its stark beauty helped inspire his passion for the old Border tales. (Courtesy Historic Scotland; P. Dougal)

Standing in a commanding position in the secluded village of Elsdon, Northumberland, is this well-preserved example of a Border tower. It was built by the Umfravilles whose coat of arms decorate the parapet wall, and since the 15th century has served as both home and refuge to Elsdon's rectors. Still inhabited today it has walls nine feet thick and features a newel staircase which leads to a battlemented walk running along three sides of the high pitched, stone tiled roof. The large windows, pierced in more settled times, give fine views over the Border hills. (P. Dougal)

existed in the Borders that in the time between the death of a sovereign and the proclamation of his or her successor, the rule of law and order became temporarily suspended. As a consequence, in the days following the death of Queen Elizabeth, which became known as 'Ill Week', the Border erupted in a spasm of violence. Taking full advantage of the short time it took to proclaim Elizabeth's heir, James VI of Scotland, as James I of England, the Grahams, Armstrongs and Elliots launched a massive raid into Cumbria, lifting nearly 5,000 cattle and sheep. Well pleased with themselves, they were little to know that they would suffer gravely for it, more so than they could ever have imagined. For that 'Ill Week' signalled what was the beginning of the end, and soon their turbulent way of life would be gone forever.

King James was determined to have a United Kingdom and one priority was to pacify the Border country and dismantle the structure of the now redundant frontier. Well aware of the depredations with which the reivers had greeted his accession to the throne, the new king on his arrival at Newcastle in April 1603, on his journey south to London, issued the following proclamation, 'to his messengers, Sheriffs and others: The late Marches and borders of the two realms of England and Scotland are now the heart of the country. Proclamation is to be made against all rebels and disorderly persons that no supply be given them, their wives or their bairnes and that they be prosecuted with fire and sword.' On reaching London he added an even more sinister footnote to the above, 'requiring all who were guilty of the foul and insolent outrages lately committed in the Borders to submit themselves to his mercy before 20th June – under penalty of being excluded from it forever'.

James further decreed that the Border Marches would cease to exist and that the office of Warden was to be abolished. He then 'prohibited the name of Borders any longer to be used, substituting in its place Middle Shires. He ordered all places of strength in those parts to be demolished except the habitation of noblemen and barons; their iron yettes to be converted into plew irnis [plough shares] and their inhabitants to betake themselves to agriculture and other works of peace.'

'Jeddart Justice'

Perhaps most significantly, James set up a Commission of ten men, five Scots and five English, to administer his policies for the pacification of the Borders. Based in Carlisle, they were given what amounted to unlimited powers. The unique Border Laws, drawn up to suit a code of violence which had been 'wynked at' by both countries in the past, were now abolished and 'if any Englishman steal in Scotland or any Scotsman steal in England any goods or cattle amounting to 12 pence he shall be punished by death'. The most blatant offenders were immediately

rounded up and served with what was known as 'Jeddart Justice', being summary execution without trial. Sir George Home was appointed to spearhead the King's crusade using whatever force he felt necessary and commenced his duties with ruthless efficiency, hanging '140 of the nimblest and most powerful thieves in all the Borders'. The reivers had endured such purges in the past, but this time their Border 'heidmen', seeing the writing on the wall, joined in the proceedings and turned zealously on their own kinsmen. Buccleuch in particular seems to have fallen to the task with enthusiasm, hanging and

This model gives a good idea of the construction and strength of the bastle or 'bastell howse' which once predominated in the Border country. Most bastles have no more than three small windows, these invariably being set high up in the wall. The wooden ladder giving access to the small, stout external door would be pulled up by the inhabitants in times of trouble. Bastles were virtually fire proof and as a further precaution stone roofing tiles were secured with sheep bones. (Border History Museum, Hexham)

drowning his erstwhile companions and drafting large numbers of them off to the 'Belgic Wars'.

Many began to believe the days of the reiver were gone forever and whilst travelling through Northumberland, one of His Majesty's judges, accompanied by his young nephew Roger North, met some of the local heidmen in Corbridge. The young man informs us that, 'They were a comical sort of people, riding upon Negs as they call their small horses; with long beards, cloaks and long broad swords with basket hilts hanging in broad belts their legs and swords almost touched the ground.' He adds, rather patronisingly, that these people 'talk'd with my Lord Judge' who was 'well pleased with their discourse'. If, as it would appear, young Roger found these people rather amusing, he was being dangerously naive, for the reiving families bitterly resented the Commission's activities. In a show of utter contempt and disregard for the forces arrayed against them, a warband of these 'comical' people, mainly Armstrongs and Elliots from Liddesdale, mounted a raid on Redesdale and inflicted the following grisly catalogue of injuries on the inhabitants. 'Lyall Robson, of the Small Burne, shott in at the harte with a single bullott, and slaine. Elizabeth Yearowe, of Stannishburne shott with twoe bullotts through both her thighes, the right thygh broken asunder with shott and slaine. Mare Robson, wyfe to James Robson called Blackehead, is shott with fyve haile shott in her breasts, Rinyon Robson of the Bellinge is shot with a bullett and an arrowe out of a long peece and hurt in the handes. Many others were shott with bullettes through their clothes, but not hurte.'

In view of this kind of behaviour, the Elliots, Armstrongs and Grahams were singled out for special attention, many eventually being exiled to Ireland where they were abandoned and forced to scrape out a living amidst the moors and bogs of Roscommon and Connaught. In addition, 150 Grahams were pressed into military service in the Low Countries where they served out their days in the English garrisons at Flushing and Brill. The turbulent folk of Tynedale and Redesdale fared no better, large numbers of them being forcibly conscripted for service in Ireland with a further 120 being sent with a Colonel Grey to fight in the Bohemian Wars. It was also stressed that the death penalty awaited any who attempted to return.

THE END OF THE REIVER

As one would expect, none of these measures, however draconian, were totally effective, and many Border stalwarts found ways of returning to their homelands. One such man was John Hall of Elsdon, in Northumberland (known as Long Parcies Jocke). In a survey of 'all notorious, lewde, idle, and misbehaved persons in Redesdale', Jocke was reported as 'returned out of Ireland by what passe we know not, a ryotous liver, ill reputed and much suspected, having nothing to maintain himself with but by keeping an alehouse'.

Old habits die hard and though their kinships were broken, and even owning a good horse and carrying weapons was prohibited, the wilder spirits kept alive the traditions of reiving and feuding. But even their numbers eventually began to dwindle, for there were fewer and fewer places left for the reiver to hide. No longer could he cross a convenient Borderline and seek sanctuary when the King's troopers galloped in hot pursuit, and in time even the majority of his own people, desperate for peace and normality, turned against him. By the 1640s what was eventually left was a hard core of 'lawless persons', being 'mosse-troupers, theifs and uthers wicked and lawless men', who, operating in well-organised gangs, terrorised the surrounding countryside by day and night with their repeated 'outrages, felonies and nefarious crymes'.

In an attempt to suppress their activities, the authorities in Northumberland reached back into the 16th century and appointed a County Keeper to enforce law and order. Based in North Tynedale – notorious for its horse thieves – he was backed up by a local peace-keeping force which was organised and paid for by local farmers and landowners. Unfortunately, it would seem this particular Keeper was in league with the moss-troopers and 'would connive at their stealing what they pleased in Scotland or in the adjacent Bishopric of Durham and would prosecute no one save those who stole from his own district'. It all sounds depressingly familiar and even though the forces of law and order 'continued to search for their haunts' and took 'all opportunities to root out and destroy them' the fugitive moss-troopers continued to skulk in the wastes of Liddesdale, Redesdale and what had been the Debateable Land, until well into the 17th century.

Even though the reiver's conduct was, in the main, deplorable and the ruthless justice eventually dealt out to him was well deserved, his martial spirit seems to have remained undaunted. It is, therefore, somewhat satisfying to hear that even as late as 1648, at the height of the Civil War, 'English Cavaliers' along with some 'Malignants of Scotland' numbering over 70 'horsemen with a small number of foot [came] to Carlisle with ladders, scaled the walls, entered the castle, broke open the gaol, released Moss troopers and other prisoners, wounded the gaoler and all marched off together into Scotland'. It must have made the 'Keen Lord Scrope' turn in his grave!

Bibliography

For those wishing to delve further into Border history, the following publications may be of interest:
J. Bain (Editor) *Calendar of Border Papers* (2 Vols 1560–1603); G. Watson *The Border Reivers*; D.L. Tough *Last Years of a Frontier*; Rev. R. Borland *Border Raids and Reivers*; G.M. Fraser *The Steel Bonnets*; R. Robson *The Rise and Fall of the English Highland Clans*; M. Robson *Ride with the Moonlight*; B. Charlton *Upper North Tynedale*; B. Charlton *The Story of Redesdale*; J. Marsden *The Illustrated Border Ballads*; C. Kightly *Flodden, the Anglo-Scottish War of 1513*; G.N. Taylor *The Story of Elsdon*; G.M. Treveleyan *The Middle Marches*; J. Prebble *Lion in the North*; R. Hugill *Borderland Castles and Peles*; B. Long *Castles of Northumberland*; A.F. Pollard *Tudor Tracts 1532–1588*.

For anyone visiting the area, the **Border History Museum** housed in the Old Gaol, Hexham, Northumberland, is well worth a visit as is the impressive display at the **Museum of Border Arms and Armour**, Teviotdale, Roxburghshire. There are many fine examples of tower houses and bastles to be seen on both sides of the Border and in the **Tullie House Museum** at Carlisle, there is an evocative audio-visual display devoted to the life and times of the Border Reiver.

An illustration from Derricke's 'The Image of Ireland' published in 1581, depicting English troops on campaign in Ireland during the period 1575–78. Officers, arquebusiers, demi-lances (middle background) and pikemen carry an interesting assortment of weapons, and five Border horsemen (top right) scout ahead. (British Library; John Tincey)

THE PLATES

A: 'Running a Foray', 1585

We witness the aftermath of a raid in the Cheviot foothills, probably in the late autumn, 'the chiefe time of stealing'. **A1**, a Border 'heidman' is well equipped for a foray. His 'steill bonnet', a burgonet, is based on an example in the Kelvin Grove Museum, Glasgow, and he wears a plain but functional back and breast over a stout slashed and padded doublet. Gauntlets, long leather riding boots and spurs complete his costume. He carries a sword of quality and, holstered forward of his saddle, a heavy, single-shot pistol known as a 'dagg'. A studded leather targe is slung from his saddle. **A2**, a Border Reiver, is clearly a veteran of countless raids and skirmishes, judging from his appearance. Under his bonnet he wears a simple steel cap known as a 'skull'; his torso being protected by a 'jack', which he wears over a tunic of heavy fustian. He carries an eight foot Border lance and a dagger. Like many Borderers, he distrusts firearms, preferring a longbow, which he carries wrapped against the weather. From his fine cloak and fashionable bonnet, **A3** could well be the heidman's son. For protection he wears a studded

brigandine and stout riding boots. In addition to his Border lance and fine sword, he carries a small but powerful hand-wound crossbow. **A4**, a 'Foot lowne' wears a sturdy cabasset, but for lightness prefers a battered breast without the back. He wears baggy breeches and carries a long ballock dagger. He is armed with a wicked looking polearm, probably fashioned from an agricultural implement.

B: Flodden Field, 1513

Flushed with the initial success of their assault on the English right flank, Highland and Lowland Scots intent on taking Sir Edmund Howard for ransom, are thwarted by the timely intervention of a troop of Border horse led by the Bastard Heron. **B1**, Sir Edmund Howard, wears outdated 'gothic' armour and defends himself with a hand-and-a-half 'bastard' sword. **B2**, a Highland Scot, wears a padded 'cotun'

Another engraving from Derricke's 'Image of Ireland' showing mail-clad Border Horse skirmishing with Irish light cavalry. Carrying steel tipped lances, the Borderers wear burgonets, stout leather riding boots and carry oval shields slung across their chests. Note the Irish cavalry's lack of stirrups and their curious, segmented helmets. In the background, axe-armed galloglasses are routed by English halberdiers and arquebusiers. (British Library; John Tincey)

and wields a fearsome double-handed 'great sword'. The ivy sprig decorating his helmet identifies him as a Gordon. **B3**, also a Highland Scot wears a cape of chainmail known as a 'Bishops Mantle'. Both the 'cotun' and 'Bishops Mantle' follow examples depicted on tombstones in the West Highlands. **B4** and **B5** are typical of the Lowland Scots who made up the bulk of James IV's army. In addition to their canvas covered jacks, thick scarves afford some protection to their necks. They were variously armed with 16 foot pikes, polearms, swords, daggers and bucklers. **B5**, the Bastard Heron, wears a studded brigandine over a mail shirt, and his helmet, a fine sallet, is blackened to prevent rusting. His war hammer is based on an example in the Wallace collection. His Borderers, carrying Lord Dacre's Red Bull Standard, are armed with lances and battleaxes and protect themselves with jacks and stout leather tunics.

C: Solway Moss, 1542

Wedged between the River Esk and the boggy Solway Moss, a column of the invading Scottish army is set upon by Thomas Wharton's mounted Cumberland 'prickers'. One of these, **C1**, discharges a 'dagg' at close range into floundering Scots infantry, **C2**, who are attempting to save a light cannon. The rider is equipped with powder and shot for his pistol and carries the key for winding up the mechanism on a long cord tied around his neck. Wearing a burgonet and a back and breast, he is well wrapped against the cold November morning. Baggy breeches tucked into leather riding boots complete his costume. **C3**, a second 'pricker', wearing a large Border bonnet, protects himself with a canvas covered jack worn over a tunic of heavy fustian. Along with his studded targe, he is equipped with a slim dagger and a Border lance. Both 'prickers' are mounted on sturdy 'hobblers' and horse trappings follow those depicted in Derricke's engravings. Note in particular the high backed saddles. The Scottish army, though seemingly well equipped, were badly led and poorly motivated. In the face of such ferocious and unexpected attacks, morale soon crumbled and the humiliating rout began.

D: 'The Hot Trod', 1590's

In response to the repeated incidents of 'maisterfull and violent theft and reafe by night and day', the 'Hot Trod' must have been a common sight along the Borderline. Borderers who had been 'spoyled' were lawfully entitled to enlist help from their neighbours and 'Trods' were allowed to cross into the opposite realm fully armed in pursuit of their stolen goods. Once across the Border, however, they were obliged to 'declare their cause' to the first person they met and ask him to 'witness the Trod'. Passing through a cluster of bastles and strong houses, this 'Trod' calls men to the 'fray' and is in 'full and freshe pursuit' with 'hound and horne, hue and crye'. The posse is led by a March Warden, **D1**, who is armoured in a

The confusion and panic overtaking the Scottish army at Solway Moss in November 1542 is clearly evident in this spirited illustration by Rick Scollins. Wielding daggs, broadswords, crossbows and Border lances, Wharton's 'prickers' wreak havoc on the Scots column. Soldiers on both sides protect themselves with a mixture of sallets, burgonets, brigandines, jacks and padded jackets. Note the mounted figure at top left who wears a simple steel 'skull' under his Border bonnet – onto which his national colours are very loosely attached! (Author's collection)

manner befitting his rank. His fine burgonet and back and breast are based on examples in the Museum of Border Arms and Armour, and he carries a pair of wheel-lock pistols holstered forward of his saddle. D2, a Trooper, carries a flaming piece of turf aloft on his spearpoint, signifying the legality of the 'Trod'. He wears a quilted leather jack and his combed morion and dagger are taken from examples in the Museum of Border Arms and Armour. Wearing a cabasset, D3, a Border rider, sounds the 'horne', and is also charged with controlling the 'slewe dogges' or hounds. Excellent trackers, these beasts were highly prized and, ironically, were often stolen by the reiving bands they were employed to catch!

E: 'A Day of Truce', 1590's

It was originally laid down in the Border laws that Warden meetings should take place every month, but records confirm that such meetings were held on an irregular basis, as and when a convenient date suited both Wardens. It had been agreed that meetings would 'not be held on the very March, for all men, ill or good, have access to armour and such numbers of deadly feud standing, it is hard to eschew brawling and bloodshed. Each Warden therefore to meet his turn with the other certain miles within his charge'. As a consequence, Wardens invariably met on or near the Borderline. These meetings, lasting from sunrise of the appointed day to sunrise of the next, were also Truce Days and during that time all persons attending were entitled to safe conduct. It was the Warden's duty to ensure the appearance of subjects from his own March against whom Bills had been filed and in addition, he would present for trial raiders from the opposing March whom he had apprehended in the course of his duties. If a Bill was 'cleaned', then the accused would go free, but if he was found guilty, and the Bill was 'fouled', punishment would be meted out or compensation paid. As well as an opportunity to gain redress for their grievances and to see justice done, Borderers also treated Truce Days as important social events. Ale flowed freely and a variety of tinkers, pedlars, musicians and travelling players turned up to ply their trade. The scene depicted here takes place in the Cheviots at Windy Gyle. E1, the English Warden, is fashionably dressed for the occasion wearing a slashed and padded doublet of quality. His Scottish counterpart, E2, not to be outdone, adds

Built in the early 14th century, this picturesque tower known as the 'Vicar's Pele' stands alongside St Andrew's Church in the village of Corbridge, Tynedale. Built with Roman worked stones pillaged from the nearby ruins of Corstopitum, it retains its original door and its interior still contains a stone table and washbasin. There are some comfortable window seats and near one of these in the west wall, there is a stone book rest, slanted so as to catch the light.

his own splash of colour to the proceedings. E3 a soberly dressed 'clark' frantically searches for a missing document, much to the mounting fury of the accused, a Border 'heidman', E4. He has retained his sword and dagger, both of which are based on examples in the Museum of Border Arms and Armour, and carries a combed morion. The proceedings are about to be disrupted by his unruly kinsmen, one of whom is about to draw a 'gonne' from beneath his cloak.

F: Ireland, 1576

During a skirmish in Ireland, a Border horseman is attacked by a Galloglass and his Kern attendant. The Borderer, F1, is wearing a burgonet, gauntlets and thigh-length mail shirt and is armed with an eight foot lance and circular shield bearing the cross of St George. F2, a Galloglass, wears an articulated burgonet and a long mail coat, worn over a saffron dyed tunic. Wielding huge double-handed swords and battleaxes, the Galloglass was usually backed up by Kerns and footsoldiers. **F3**, a Kern, sports a 'glib' hairstyle – peculiarly Irish and outlawed by the English – and wears a full, saffron dyed shirt gathered at the waist. The Celtic designs on his short doublet further emphasise his Gaelic origins. Fighting barefoot, he is armed with a crude light polearm.

G: The Rescue of Kinmont Willie, 1596

'Kinmont' Willie Armstrong was a notable villain who had strong connections on both sides of the Border. He married into the Graham family and was also a tenant and ally of the powerful Maxwells. His notorious gang, known as 'Kinmont's Bairns', included some of the most desperate ruffians in the Debateable Land. For years they plundered with impunity in both England and Scotland, eluding the Scottish King's troopers and evading the clutches of Henry, Lord Scrope, Warden of the English West March. In 1596 however, whilst Kinmont was returning home from a Truce Day, Salkeld, Scrope's deputy, frustrated to the point of desperation by the reivers' atrocities, took Kinmont prisoner and incarcerated him in Carlisle castle. This act was in clear contravention of Border laws. Walter Scott of Buccleuch then Keeper of Liddesdale, on whose territory the arrest had been made, protested violently about the incident, demanding Kinmont's release. Scrope however simply refused to free 'such a malefactor'. After much heated correspondence, Buccleuch decided to break Kinmont free by force of arms. The rescue was planned at a horse race at Langholm, and on the night of 13 April 1596 a force of Elliots, Scotts, Armstrongs and Grahams gathered at Morton in the Debateable Land. Led by Buccleuch, the raiding party included such notable freebooters as Auld Wat of Harden, Will Elliot the Goodman of Gorrombye, the Lairds of Goldielandes and Todrigg, Willie 'Redcloak' Bell and one Ally, a bastard. The dark and rainy night provided perfect cover and the raiding party soon covered the ten miles to Carlisle. A vanguard of about 30–40 men led the way, equipped with crowbars and ladders, followed by the main assault group led by Buccleuch. A further group brought up the rear and were positioned to cover a retreat if things went badly. Crossing the dangerously flooded river Eden, the raiders arrived at Carlisle Castle only to find their ladders were too short to scale the walls! Undaunted, they found a small postern door in the west wall and quickly undermined it. Due to the appalling weather, the castle watch had retired indoors and Buccleuch and his men were soon inside the castle undetected. It was reported that Buccleuch was the fifth man to enter and encouraged his men with these words: Stand to yt, for I have vowed to God and my prince that I would fetch oute of England Kynmont dead or quicke, and will maintaine that accion when it is donn, with fyre and sworde against all resisters'. There is little doubt that Buccleuch had allies inside the castle, for he and his men quickly found the chamber where Kinmont was being held. Though the alarm had now been raised the raiders, carrying Kinmont Willie with them, were soon out of the castle and, covered by the rearguard, swiftly crossed the Eden making their way to Scotland and safety. The incident caused a scandal on both sides of the Border and Buccleuch was eventually hauled before Queen Elizabeth and asked how he had dared to break into her castle. Buccleuch reputedly replied 'What, madam, is there that a brave man may not dare?', a reply which evidently pleased Her Majesty as he was subsequently allowed to return home unharmed! The plate shows Buccleuch, **G1**, greeting Kinmont, **G2**, as he is carried out of captivity by the huge reiver known as Red Rowan, **G3**. Watchful reivers, **G4** and **G5**, stand guard while others beckon them into the darkness beyond.

H: Moss troopers, 1603

When the antiquarian William Camden visited the Roman Wall at Busy Gap, near Housesteads, in 1599, he found that the area was 'a place infamous for thieving and robbing' and that he 'could not with safety take a full survey . . . for the rank robbers thereabouts'. It would appear that Moss troopers actually adapted places of strength along the wall and used them as bases for their own depradations. Near such a place, and about to ambush a party of travellers, are three Moss troopers. **H1**, wears a 'combed' morion and his crude back and breast has been blackened to avoid rusting. He holds a primed 'dagg' and carries an additional pair holstered and ready for use. **H2**, wears a 'Spanish' morion and relies on a stout slashed and padded tunic for protection. He too

arries a brace of 'daggs', but still retains his longbow
n case of emergency. **H3**, is aiming a heavy
matchlock musket. Wearing a studded leather jerkin
for protection, he carries a good supply of powder
and shot slung from his bandolier. Their desperation
reflects the waning fortunes of such robber bands.

A Graham stronghold on the River Lyne, Brackenhill tower stands four and half miles east of Longtown. Dating from 1586, its walls are five feet thick and rise to a height of forty feet. Its double gabled roof is surrounded by a corbelled and battlemented parapet and its windows have iron grilles set into them. Built in the heart of robber territory, it stood perilously between the Debateable Land and the Bewcastle Wastes and was accordingly strengthened by 'Richie' Graham, a freebooter who used it as a base for his own depredations.
(P. Armstrong)

Notes sure les planches en couleur

A: 'Un Raid', 1585
Cette scène décrit les suites d'un raid. **A1**, un 'heidman' des Borders, porte une bourguignotte, plastron et dossière, sur un doublet à crevés et rembourré, des gantelets, des bottes de cheval en cuir et des éperons. Il est armé, entre autres, d'une épée, d'un lourd pistolet à un coup et d'un bouclier de cuir à clous, que l'on appelle targe. **A2** et un Border Reiver vétéran. Sous son bonnet, il porte un simple casque d'acier. Son torse est protégé par un 'jack' et il porte une lance des Borders de huit pieds et un poignard. Il porte son arquebuse dans un fourreau pour la protéger des intempéries. **A3** pourrait bien être le fils du heidman. Ses vêtements sont à la mode mais pratiques. En plus de sa lance des Borders et de son épée, il porte une petite arquebuse puissante. **A4**, un 'Foot lowne', porte un solide casque cabasset, un plastron martelé sans dossière sans dos et est armé d'une hallebarde.

B: Flodden Field, 1513
Les plans de ces Ecossais des Highlands et des Lowlands, qui désiraient prendre Sir Edmund Howard en otage, sont contrariés par l'intervention bienvenue d'une troupe de cavaliers des Borders sous la direction du Bastard Heron. **B1**, Sir Edmund Howard, porte une armure 'gothique' et se défend avec une épée 'bâtarde' d'une main et demie. **B2**, un Ecossais des Highlands, porte un 'cotun' rembourré et manie une impressionnante 'grande épée' à deux poignées. **B3**, également un Ecossais des Highlands, porte une cape en cotte de mailles nommée 'Manteau d'Evêque'. **B4** et **B5** sont des exemples typiques des Ecossais des Lowlands qui remplissaient les rangs de l'armée de Jacques IV. **B6**, le Bastard Heron, porte une brigandine à clous sur une chemise en cotte de mailles et une belle salade. Il porte un maillotin alors que ses Borderers sont armés de lances et haches d'armes.

C: Solway Moss, 1542
Une colonne de l'armée écossaise est attaquée par des 'prickers' montés. L'un d'entre eux, **C1**, décharge un pistolet à courte portée dans l'infanterie écossaise en déroute. **C2**. Le cavalier porte une bourguignotte, un plastron et dossière et des culottes larges rentrées dans des bottes de cheval en cuir. **C3**, un second 'pricker' porte un grand bonnet des Borders et un 'jack' recouvert de toile. Les deux sont montés sur de solides 'hobblers'. Notez en particulier les selles à dosseret.

D: 'Le Trod'
Le 'Trod' permettait aux Borderers qui avaient essuyé un raid de passer en royaume ennemi entièrement armés pour récupérer les objets qui leur avaient été volés. Ce groupe est sous la direction d'un March Warden, **D1**, dont l'armure correspond au rang. **D2**, un cavalier, porte un morceau de tourbe enflammé à la pointe de sa lance pour indiquer la légalité du 'Trod'. **D3**, un cavalier des Borders souffle dans le 'horne' et est également responsable du contrôle de la meute.

Farbtafeln

A: "Auf einem Streifzug", 1585
Diese Szene zeigt das Nachspiel eines Überfalls. **A1**, ein "heidman" im Grenzgebiet zwischen England und Schottland, trägt eine Sturmhaube, Rücken- und Brustschutz über einem zerfetzten, gepolsterten Wams, Stulpenhandschuhe, Reitstiefel aus Leder und Sporen. Zu seinen Waffen zählen ein Schwert, ein schweres Einzelschußgewehr und ein beschlagener Lederschild, der Tartsche genannt wird. **A2** zeigt einen Veteran der Border Reivers. Unter seiner Mütze trägt er eine einfache Stahlkappe; sein Oberkörper wird von einem sogenannten "jack", einer Panzerjacke, geschützt. Er hat eine 2,5m lange Border-Lanze und einen Dolch bei sich. Sein Langbogen wurde eingewickelt, um ihn vor dem Wetter zu schützen. Bei **A3** könnte es sich um den Sohn des "heidman" handeln. Seine Kleidung ist recht modisch, doch durchaus praktisch. Zusätzlich zu seiner Border-Lanze und seinem Schwert trägt er eine kleine, doch leistungsfähige Armbrust. Der "Foot lowne" **A4** trägt einen robusten "Cabasset"-Helm, eine lädierte Brustplatte ohne Rücken und ist mit einer Stangenwaffe ausgestattet.

B: Flodden Field, 1513
Highland- und Lowland-Schotten mit dem Plan, Sir Edmund Howard gefangenzunehmen und Lösegeld zu verlangen. Ihr Vorhaben wird jedoch durch das rechtzeitige Einschreiten einer Border-Reitertruppe, die von "Bastard Heron" angeführt wird, zerschlagen. **B1**: Sir Edmund Howard trägt den "gotischen" Panzer und verteidigt sich mit einem anderthalb Hand langen "Bastard"-Schwert. **B2**: Highland-Schotte in einem gepolsterten "cotun", der ein mächtiges zweihändiges "Großschwert" schwingt. **B3**: Auch ein Highland-Schotte, der einen Kettenumhang trägt, der den Beinamen "Bischofsmantel" hat. **B4** und **B5** sind Abbildungen typischer Lowland-Schotten, die den Großteil der Streitkraft von James IV. ausmachten. **B6**: "Bastard Heron" in einem beschlagenen Panzerhemd über einem Kettenhemd und einer schönen Schallern. Er hat einen Streithammer bei sich, seine Borderers sind mit Lanzen und Streitäxten bewaffnet.

C: Solway Moss, 1542
Eine Kolonne der einmarschierenden schottischen Armee wird von berittenen "prickers" überfallen, von denen einer - **C1** - aus nächster Nähe eine Pistole auf die sich abmühende schottische Infanterie abfeuert. **C2**: Der Reiter trägt eine Sturmhaube, Rücken- und Brustschutz sowie lose Kniehosen, die in Reitstiefel aus Leder gesteckt sind. **C3**: Ein zweiter "pricker" mit einer großen Border-Mütze und einer mit Segeltuch überzogenen Panzerjacke. Beide reiten robuste "hobblers". Man beachte besonders die Sättel mit hohem Rücken.

D: "The Hot Trod"
Der "Trod" ermöglichte es den Borderers, die überfallen worden waren, das Reich

E: 'Un jour de trève', vers 1590

Les lois des Borders indiquaient à l'origine que les Wardens devaient se réunir tous les mois mais les documents confirment que ces réunions étaient organisées de manière irrégulière. La scène décrite ici se déroule dans les Cheviots, à Windy Gyle. E1, le Warden anglais, et E2, le Warden écossais, sont tous les deux habillés à la mode pour l'occasion. E3, un 'clark' sobrement vêtu, cherche désespérément un document manquant, à la grande colère de l'accusé, un 'heidman' des Borders, E4.

F: Irlande, 1576

Durant une échauffourée en Irlande, un cavalier des Borders est attaqué par un Galloglass et son assistant Kern. Le Borderer, F1, porte une bourguignotte, des gantelets et une cotte de maille qui descend jusqu'aux cuisses. Il est armé d'une lance de huit pieds et d'un bouclier circulaire qui porte la croix de saint Georges. F2, un Galloglass, porte une bourguignotte articulée, une longue cotte de mailles et porte une énorme épée à deux poignées. La coupe de cheveux de F3, un Kern ou fantassin, est spécifique à l'Irlande. Les motifs celtes de son doublet soulignent encore plus ses origines gaéliques.

G: La délivrance de Kinmont Willie, 1596

'Kinmont' Willie Armstrong était un bandit notoire qui dirigeait un groupe de bandits. Pillant avec impunité, il fut arrêté et incarcéré au château de Carlisle. Mais son arrestation se produisit dans des circonstances totalement opposées aux lois des Borders. Walter Scott de Buccleuth protesta et exigea qu'on relâche Kinmont. Lord Scrope, Warden du English March, refusa et, après une longue correspondance animée, Buccleuth décida de libérer Kinmont par la force. Cette expédition était bien préparée. De nombreux pillards notables y participèrent. Une nuit sombre et pluvieuse représentait une parfaite occasion et Buccleuth et ses hommes se trouvèrent vite dans le château sans être aperçus. Bien que l'alarme ait été donnée, la bande, qui s'était emparée de Kinmont Willie, ne mit pas longtemps à sortir du château et à retraverser la frontière pour se retrouver en sécurité. Cet incident provoqua un scandale des deux côtés de la frontière et c'est l'un des plus célèbres de l'histoire des Borders. Cette planche dépeint Buccleuth, G1, qui salue Kinmont, G2, alors que l'énorme reiver connu sous le nom de Red Rowan, G3, le sort de sa prison. Des reivers, G4, et G5, montent la garde alors que d'autres leur font signe au loin.

H: Cavaliers Moss, 1603

Trois cavaliers Moss ont tendu une embuscade à un groupe de voyageurs. H1 porte un morion 'peigné' et un plastron et dossière rudimentaire. H2 porte un morion 'espagnol' et porte deux pistolets. H3 vise avec un lourd mousquet à mèche. Leur désespoir reflète le déclin des fortunes de ces bandes de voleurs.

des Gegners voll bewaffnet zu betreten und zu versuchen, die gestohlenen Güte zurückzugewinnen. Diese Schar wird von einem Markaufseher - D1 - angefüh der eine Rüstung trägt, die seinem Rang entspricht. D2: Ein Soldat trägt ei brennendes Stück Torf auf der Spitze seines Speers, was die Rechtmäßigkeit de "Trod" bezeichnen soll. D3: Der Reiter der Borderers bläst das "horne" und ist auch für die Hundemeute verantwortlich.

E: "Ein Tag der Waffenruhe", 90er Jahre des 16. Jh.

Ursprünglich war in den Gesetzen für das Grenzgebiet zwischen England und Schottland festgelegt worden, daß sich die Aufseher regelmäßig einmal im Monat treffen sollten. Aufzeichnungen ist jedoch zu entnehmen, daß diese Zusammenkünfte in unregelmäßigen Zeitabständen stattfanden. Die hier abgebildete Szene spielt sich in den Cheviots in Windy Gyle ab. E1, der englische Aufseher, und E2, der schottische Aufseher, sind beide dem Anlaß entsprechend modisch gekleidet. E3: Ein unauffällig gekleideter "Schreiber", der verzweifelt nach einem fehlenden Schriftstück sucht, was den Angeklagten - einen Border "heidman" (E4) - sichtlich in Wut versetzt.

F: Irland, 1576

Bei einem Scharmützel in Irland wird ein Reiter der Borderers von einem Galloglass und seinem Gefolgsmann der Kerns angegriffen. Der Borderer, F1, trägt eine Sturmhaube, Stulpenhandschuhe und ein schenkellanges Kettenhemd. Er ist mit einer 2,5m langen Lanze und einem Rundschild bewaffnet, auf dem das Kreuz von St. George zu erkennen ist. F2: Der Galloglass trägt eine Glieder-Sturmhaube, einen langen Kettenmantel und hat ein riesiges zweihändiges Schwert bei sich. F3: Der Fußsoldat der Kerns hat eine typisch irische Frisur, und das keltische Muster auf seinem Wams betont seine gälische Herkunft weiter.

G: Die Befreiung von Kinmont Willie, 1596

"Kinmont" Willie Armstrong war ein bekannter Bösewicht und Anführer einer Bande verwegener Schurken. Er plünderte ungestraft, wurde dann jedoch verhaftet und in der Burg von Carlisle eingesperrt. Seine Festnahme stellte jedoch einen eindeutigen Verstoß gegen die Gesetze für das Grenzgebiet zwischen England und Schottland dar. Walter Scott of Buccleuch protestierte gegen diesen Vorfall und forderte seine Freilassung. Lord Scrope, der Aufseher der englischen Mark, weigerte sich, dieser Forderung stattzugeben. Im Anschluß an mehrere wütende Schreiben beschloß Buccleuch, Kinmont mit Gewalt zu befreien. Die Aktion war bis aufs Kleinste durchdacht, und viele bekannte Freibeuter beteiligten sich daran. Im Schutz einer dunklen, regnerischen Nacht gelangten Buccleuch und seine Helfer unentdeckt in das Innere der Burg. Obgleich Alarm geschlagen wurde, konnten die Reiber mit Kinmont Willie entkommen und sich auf der anderen Seite der Grenze in Sicherheit bringen. Der Vorfall verursachte auf beiden Seiten der Grenze einen Skandal, und gehört noch heute zu den berühmtesten Ereignissen in der Geschichte des Grenzgebiets. Die Farbtafel zeigt Buccleuch, G1, wie er Kinmont, G2, begrüßt und dieser von dem hünenhaften "reiver" mit dem Beinamen "Red Rowan", G3, aus seinem Gefängnis getragen wird. Wachsame "reivers", G4 und G5, halten Wache, während andere sie zu sich in sichere Entfernung winken.

H: Moss-Soldaten, 1603

Drei Moss-Soldaten wollen gerade eine Gruppe von Reisenden überfallen. H1 trägt eine Sturmhaube "mit Kamm" sowie dürftigen Rücken- und Brustschutz. H2 trägt eine "spanische" Sturmhaube und hat ein Pistolenpaar bei sich. H3 legt eine schwere Luntenmuskete an. Ihre Verwegenheit verdeutlicht das schlechter werdende Schicksal solcher Räuberbanden.